STEEL MAGNOLIAS

BY ROBERT HARLING

★

DRAMATISTS
PLAY SERVICE
INC.

NOTE ON BILLING

SPECIAL NOTE ON SONGS/RECORDINGS

In Memory of
Susan Harling Robinson.
Dedicated to her son,
Robert.

STEEL MAGNOLIAS was originally presented at the WPA Theatre (Kyle Renick, Artistic Director; Wendy Bustard, Managing Director) in New York City on March 22, 1987. It was directed by Pamela Berlin; the setting was by Edward T. Gianfrancesco; the lighting was by Craig Evans; the costumes were by Don Newcomb; the sound was by Otts Munderloh; the hair was by Bobby H. Grayson; the casting was by Darlene Kaplan; and the production stage manager was Paul Mills Holmes. The cast, in order of appearance, was as follows:

TRUVY .... Margo Martindale
ANNELLE .... Constance Shulman
CLAIREE .... Kate Wilkinson
SHELBY .... Blanche Baker
M'LYNN .... Rosemary Prinz
OUISER .... Mary Fogarty

The WPA Theatre production of STEEL MAGNOLIAS was transferred by special arrangement with Lucille Lortel to the Lucille Lortel Theatre on June 19, 1987. It was directed by Pamela Berlin; the setting was by Edward T. Gianfrancesco; the lighting was by Craig Evans; the costumes were by Don Newcomb; the hair design and supervision was by Bobby H. Grayson; the sound was by Aural Fixation; and the production stage manager was Cosmo P. Hanson. The cast, in order of appearance, was as follows:

TRUVY .... Margo Martindale
ANNELLE .... Constance Shulman
CLAIREE .... Kate Wilkinson
SHELBY .... Betsy Aidem
M'LYNN .... Rosemary Prinz
OUISER .... Mary Fogarty

Place: Chinquapin, Louisiana
  ACT ONE: SCENE I: April
                SCENE II: December
  ACT TWO: SCENE I: June, eighteen months later
                SCENE II: November

CAST OF CHARACTERS

TRUVY JONES — 40ish. Owner of the beauty shop.

ANNELLE DUPUY-DESOTO — 19. Beauty shop assistant.

CLAIREE BELCHER — 66ish. Widow of former mayor. Grande dame.

SHELBY EATENTON-LATCHERIE — 25. Prettiest girl in town.

M'LYNN EATENTON — 50ish. Shelby's mother. Socially prominent career woman.

OUISER (pronounced "Weezer") BOUDREAUX — 66ish. Wealthy curmudgeon. Acerbic but loveable.

AUTHOR'S NOTE: The women in this play are witty, intelligent, and above all, real characters. They in no way, shape or form are meant to be portrayed as cartoons or caricatures.

STEEL MAGNOLIAS

ACT ONE

SCENE I

The curtain rises on Truvy's beauty shop. There are the sounds of gunshots and a dog barking. Annelle is spraying Truvy's hair with more hair spray than necessary.

ANNELLE. Oops! I see a hole.

TRUVY. I was hoping you'd catch that.

ANNELLE. It's a little poofier than I would normally do, but I'm nervous.

TRUVY. I'm not real concerned about that. When I go to bed I wrap my entire head with toilet tissue so it usually gets a little smushed down anyway in that process.

ANNELLE. In my class at the trade school, I was number one when it came to frosting and streaking. I did my own.

TRUVY. Really? I wouldn't have known. And I can spot a bottle job at twenty paces. *(Studying her hairdo.)* Well…your technique is good, and your form and content will improve with experience. So, you're hired.

ANNELLE. *(Overcome.)* Oh!!

TRUVY. And not a moment too soon! This morning we're going to be as busy as a one-armed paper hanger.

ANNELLE. Thank you, Miss Truvy! Thank you…

TRUVY. No time. Now. You know where the coffee stuff is. Everything else is on a tray next to the stove. *(Truvy removes her smock.)*

ANNELLE. Here. Let me help you. *(Dusts her off.)* You've got little tiny hairs and fuzzies all over you.

TRUVY. Honey, there's so much static electricity in here I pick up everything except boys and money. *(Points Annelle toward the kitchen.)* Be a treasure. *(Annelle exits into the kitchen. Truvy immediately starts redoing her hairdo.)* Annelle? This is the most successful shop in town. Wanna know why?

ANNELLE. *(Offstage.)* Why?

TRUVY. Because I have a strict philosophy that I have stuck to for fifteen years…"There is no such thing as natural beauty." That's why I've never lost a client to the Kut and Kurt or the Beauty Box. And remember! My ladies get only the best. Do not scrimp on anything. Feel free to use as much hair spray as you want. *(Annelle returns with the tray. The sound of a gunshot makes her jump, but she recovers.)* Just shove that stuff to one side, it goes right there. *(Pointing out the room.)* Manicure station here…

ANNELLE. There's no such thing as natural beauty…

TRUVY. Remember that, or we're all out of a job. Just look at me, Annelle. It takes some effort to look like this.

ANNELLE. I can see that. How many ladies do we have this morning?

TRUVY. I restrict myself to the ladies of the neighborhood on Saturday mornings. Normally that would be just three, but today we've got Shelby Eatenton. She's not a regular, she's the daughter of a regular. I have to do something special with her hair. She's getting married this afternoon. Now. How long have you been here in town?

ANNELLE. A few weeks…

TRUVY. New in town! It must be exciting being in a new place. I wouldn't know. I've lived here all my life.

ANNELLE. It's a little scary.

TRUVY. I can imagine. Well…tell me things about yourself.

ANNELLE. There's nothing to tell. I live here. I've got a job now. That's it. Could I borrow a few of these back issues of *Southern Hair*?

TRUVY. Uh…sure. It's essential to keep abreast of the latest styles. I'm glad to see your interest. I get *McCall's, Family Circle, Glamour, Mademoiselle, Ladies' Home Journal*, every magazine known to man. You must live close by. Within walking distance, I mean. I didn't see a car.

ANNELLE. My car's... I don't have a car. I've been staying across the river at Robeline's Boarding House.

TRUVY. That's quite a walk. Ruth Robeline...now there's a story. She's a twisted, troubled soul. Her life has been an experiment in terror. Husband killed in World War II. Her son was killed in Vietnam. I have to tell you, when it comes to suffering, she's right up there with Elizabeth Taylor.

ANNELLE. I had no idea. *(There is a loud gunshot and barking.)* Is that a gunshot?

TRUVY. Yes, dear. I believe it is. Plug in the hotplate, please.

ANNELLE. But why is someone firing a gun in a nice neighborhood like this?

TRUVY. It's a long story. It has to do with Shelby's wedding and her father. *(More gunfire and barking.)* You'll be happier if you just ignore it like the rest of the neighborhood.

CLAIREE. *(Entering.)* Knock, knock!

TRUVY. Morning, Clairee!

CLAIREE. Morning, Truvy.

TRUVY. I tried to call you and tell you I was running late. No answer.

CLAIREE. I was at the high school. I was out at the crack of dawn.

TRUVY. Annelle, I want you to meet the former first lady of Chinquapin, Mrs. Belcher. Clairee, this is Annelle. She's taking Judy's place.

ANNELLE. Pleased to meet you.

CLAIREE. I'm a little embarrassed. If I had known I was meeting new people, I would have taken a little more pride in my appearance. I have been at the dedication of our new football field. I am not always this windblown.

TRUVY. Annelle. They named the stadium after her late husband... Lloyd Belcher Memorial Coliseum. The team has voted her all sorts of special titles.

CLAIREE. I have the pom-poms to prove it. What is your name, dear?

ANNELLE. Oh. My married name's Dupuy.

CLAIREE. I don't think I know any Dupuys.

ANNELLE. I just moved here. I'm originally from Zwolle.

CLAIREE. That explains it. Truvy? I thought I brought you those recipes. *(She fumbles with her shirt that has no pockets.)*

TRUVY. Clairee. The reason I called is, do you mind if I do Shelby first?

CLAIREE. That's fine. I'll amuse myself. Shelby's the most important one today. *(A gunshot.)* That man! I'll swanee...I think the situation is worse than ever.

TRUVY. Annelle? We're going to need more towels. They're stacked up next to the washing machine. *(Annelle exits.)*

CLAIREE. Sweet girl. Where'd you find her?

TRUVY. She heard I had a position open and she just walked in. I think there's a story here.

CLAIREE. What makes you say that?

TRUVY. For starters. She's married...but she lives at Ruth Robeline's. *(Clairee reacts.)* Alone.

CLAIREE. I'd get to the bottom of this, if I were you. You have some nice silverware you'd like to keep.

TRUVY. Oh, I'm not worried about that. She's very nice. I just love the idea of hiring someone with a past.

CLAIREE. She can't be more than eighteen. She hasn't had time to have a past.

TRUVY. Honey. It's the eighties. If you can achieve puberty, you can achieve a past.

CLAIREE. *(Annelle enters, carrying towels. Clairee sips her coffee and grimaces.)* Yuck! *(Truvy, concerned, takes a sip.)*

TRUVY. Annelle? How did you make this coffee?

ANNELLE. Like you said. I poured hot water through the thing.

TRUVY. Where'd you get the water?

ANNELLE. It was boiling on the stove.

TRUVY. Did you notice the hot dogs in the bottom of the pot?

ANNELLE. No.

TRUVY. Make some more, please.

ANNELLE. I'm so sorry.

CLAIREE. Don't worry. I love a good hot dog. Just not with cream and sugar. *(Annelle exits.)*

TRUVY. She's probably not an international spy. But! If she works out, I may let her rent the garage apartment.

CLAIREE. I thought the twins were going to live there while they go to the college.

TRUVY. Recent developments. Louie's going away to LSU now. And Poot has decided to work for my cousin in Baltimore. He doesn't want to be called Poot anymore. My babies are growing up.

CLAIREE. I can't believe your kids are old enough to leave the nest.

TRUVY. You know I was a child bride. Well. I look at the bright side. I have some places to visit now. I've always wanted to go to Baltimore. I'm told it's the hairdo capital of the world.

CLAIREE. *(Finding the recipes in her pocket.)* Here they are! I'm so fat I couldn't feel them.

TRUVY. The recipes? Let me see... *(Truvy takes the recipe cards and pores over them. Clairee reads over her shoulder.)* Um...this sounds delicious.

CLAIREE. It is. And the Bisquick makes it so simple. *(Pulls another card.)* And this is from my daughter-in-law. She says you can't attend a function in Tickfaw where this is not served.

TRUVY. Yum. *(Reading.)* Now are these chocolate chips semi-sweet or milk?

CLAIREE. Milk.

TRUVY. Is the Karo syrup light or dark?

CLAIREE. Matter of taste.

TRUVY. Where's that other one you were telling me about... Cuppa, cuppa, cuppa?

CLAIREE. That's so easy you don't have to write it down. Cup of flour, cup of sugar, cup of fruit cocktail with the juice. Mix it up and bake at 350 'til gold and bubbly.

TRUVY. Sounds awfully rich.

CLAIREE. It is. So I serve it over ice cream to cut the sweetness. Give me some paper, I'll copy them down for you.

TRUVY. *(Calling.)* Annelle? Get Miss Clairee some paper. I believe there's some stuck on the Frigidaire under the crawfish. *(To Clairee.)* Oh…and here's that article on Princess Di. *(There are gunshots and frenzied barking.)* Sometimes I wonder if Drum Eatenton's brain gets enough oxygen. That is so annoying.

CLAIREE. Try living next door to him. *(Enter Shelby. Her hair is in rollers. She carries a picture torn out of a magazine. She is a blushing bride in the first stages of completion.)*

SHELBY. Hi, everybody!

TRUVY. There she is! There's my girl! Come break my neck. *(Shelby's fingernails are wet, so she is careful when she hugs.)*

SHELBY. Truvy. It's so good to see you! Morning, Miss Clairee! It's not that I'm unfriendly, I'm just worried about my nails.

TRUVY. What a pretty color.

SHELBY. I hope this doesn't dry too dark. If it's too dark, it will never do. You know the colors are never the same on the bottle.

TRUVY. You will always find that to be true.

SHELBY. *(Her nails.)* This is drying way too dark. "Practically Pink" my foot! Truvy? Do you have any of those nail polish remover things?

TRUVY. *(Handing her some.)* Here. Where's your mama?

SHELBY. Right behind me, I thought. *(Annelle enters with fresh coffee.)* Hi! I'm Shelby Eatenton…soon to be Latcherie.

ANNELLE. Hi. I'm Annelle. I'm new.

TRUVY. Today's Annelle's first day.

SHELBY. Well, Annelle. You're working with the best. Anyone who's anybody gets their hair done at Truvy's.

TRUVY. Absolutely. *(A loud series of gunshots.)* Shelby…uh you know I would walk on my lips to avoid criticizing anyone but your father is about to make us all pull our hair out. And that is bad for my business.

SHELBY. Well, he should be finished with his yard work soon.

TRUVY. I hope so.

SHELBY. You're not the only one concerned. Mama's about to have a fit. She and Daddy are fighting like cats and dogs.

CLAIREE. They're just anxious with so much going on.

SHELBY. No they're not. They just try to create as much tension as possible in any given situation. It's a creed they live by.

TRUVY. You know. I was just reading an article in *Glamour* about tension during family occasions. It seems there can be a lot of stress and trauma. The thing I found most interesting is that stressful times can unleash deep dark hostilities that make your hair fall out.

SHELBY. They're fighting about patio furniture. Jackson and I will never fight about silly things. Are you married, Annelle?

ANNELLE. *(Changing subject.)* Oh. I hope that coffee's better.

CLAIREE. It smells right.

ANNELLE. *(Looking at the picture Shelby brought.)* How pretty...

SHELBY. Princess Grace...

TRUVY. Did you bring me the picture of that hairdo like I asked?

SHELBY. Here you go. Study it carefully. *(Pulls out a plastic bag.)* Here's the baby's breath.

TRUVY. This is so exciting. I feel like I am present at the creation. There is something so wondrous about the way a bride looks. I feel it is beauty in its purest form. *(Studying the picture and the bag of baby's breath.)* Where are you going to put this stuff? There's no baby's breath in this picture.

SHELBY. You just stick it in. It's meant to frame my face. Baby's breath is part of my whole decoration concept. For a total romantic look. *(Notices Clairee's shoes.)* Miss Clairee! What cute shoes!

CLAIREE. You think so? I'm not so sure. I think they're a little too racy for me. I'll probably give them away.

TRUVY. Ooo. Those are too cha-cha for words. If you decide to get rid of them, I'll buy 'em from you.

CLAIREE. What size do you wear?

TRUVY. Well. In a good shoe, I wear a size six, but sevens feel so good, I buy a size eight.

CLAIREE. They're eight and a halfs.

TRUVY. Perfect. *(M'Lynn enters carrying a large tote bag.)*

SHELBY. Hi, Mama. Look at Miss Clairee's shoes.

TRUVY. Ah, ah, ah! They're mine!

M'LYNN. Is this a riddle?

SHELBY. Annelle. This is my mama. How're things at the house?

M'LYNN. Fine. Ouiser Boudreaux just this second dropped by to talk to your father. One or both of them is probably lying in a pool of blood by now. *(To Annelle.)* Hello. Did you say Annelle? What a pretty name. Unusual. I'm M'Lynn.

TRUVY. How's the mother of the bride?

M'LYNN. Don't ask.

TRUVY. What's the matter?

M'LYNN. Nothing a handful of prescription drugs couldn't take care of.

ANNELLE. I'll take this for you. *(Annelle takes M'Lynn's bag.)*

M'LYNN. Just put it over there, please. *(Annelle puts it near Clairee.)*

TRUVY. Annelle. Why don't you go on and shampoo Mrs. Eatenton? These girls have mountains to move today.

M'LYNN. Ain't that the truth.

TRUVY. Her coiffure card is right on top.

ANNELLE. *(Looking at the card.)* Oh. Piece of cake.

SHELBY. Mama. This color is all wrong. It looks like a stuck pig bled all over my hands.

M'LYNN. I'm sure I have something at the house that'll do.

SHELBY. But do you have pink?

M'LYNN. Of course I have pink.

SHELBY. It has to be delicate.

M'LYNN. If I don't have something, we'll send one of the boys to get you some delicate pink nail polish.

SHELBY. Great idea, Mama. I'd love to see what Tommy'd pick out.

CLAIREE. Anything I can do to help out last minute?

M'LYNN. You've done plenty, Clairee. I think we've got everything situated. We've just finished borrowing every fern in North

Louisiana. The boys got in last night and they're taking care of the odds and ends.

CLAIREE. I hope the rain holds off. I'm sorry it's not a prettier day.

SHELBY. This is perfect weather for me. I don't function well when it's hot. I love cloudy days. On cloudy days I feel God's not trying very hard, so I don't have to either.

M'LYNN. She does sweat profusely.

SHELBY. Thank you, Mama.

TRUVY. Heat never bothers me. I love it. But spicy foods make me sweat. Especially on the top of my head. My hair gets wet. *(The phone rings.)*

CLAIREE. I'll get it.

M'LYNN. I'll bet that's for me. It's probably my mind trying to locate my body.

CLAIREE. *(Answering.)* Hello? Yessir, she is. Hold on a minute. M'Lynn. It's your husband.

M'LYNN. *(Takes phone.)* Yes Drum? I don't know. I haven't got it. I don't have it. Drum, if you're trying to drive me crazy, you're too late. For the last time...I don't have it. Ask the boys. Goodbye. *(She hangs up.)*

SHELBY. What did Daddy want?

M'LYNN. Nothing.

TRUVY. *(Looking at the picture and at Shelby's hair...)* So...we want to sweep it up, but leave some softness around your ears...

M'LYNN. Sweep it up?

SHELBY. Yes, Mama. Up. Like Princess Grace.

M'LYNN. Did you bring Truvy the picture of Jaclyn Smith?

SHELBY. No. I brought the picture of Princess Grace. I destroyed the picture of Jaclyn Smith.

M'LYNN. But I thought I had made you understand the advantages of the Jaclyn Smith hairdo...

SHELBY. No, Mama.

M'LYNN. Well. At least I talked her out of that stupid idea of sticking that baby's breath all in her hair.

15

SHELBY. Keep your head in the sink, please. *(Annelle accidentally squirts M'Lynn.)*

ANNELLE. *(Bringing M'Lynn up.)* I'm sorry. I'm so sorry.

M'LYNN. That's all right. I find cold water refreshing. It startled me a little, that's all.

CLAIREE. Truvy? Could I copy your recipe for Strawberry Pie?

TRUVY. Sure. *(Clairee gets the recipe box. Truvy works on Shelby's hair.)* Your mother doesn't tell us much, Shelby. What's Jackson like?

SHELBY. He's pretty swell. I thought he was a pest at first, but then he kind of grew on me. And now I love him.

TRUVY. Where'd you meet him?

SHELBY. At a party at the Petroleum Club in Shreveport. I had no idea who he was, but I was getting a big kick out of watching him on the dance floor. It was painfully obvious he had never taken the time to dance in front of a mirror. There was something so attractive about how stupid he looked.

TRUVY. Is he real romantic?

SHELBY. No. But he does give me flowers. And little presents if I bug him enough. He has promised to give me a red rose on every anniversary corresponding to the number of that anniversary. I think that's so sweet.

TRUVY. Well, now. That's a pretty romantic idea, isn't it?

SHELBY. Yes. I wish it had been his.

CLAIREE. Lloyd and I missed it to fifty years by three months. That stinker. Bless his heart. He tried. He just couldn't make it.

SHELBY. You remember your wedding?

CLAIREE. Of course I do. I remember everything. The flowers, the food. Ouiser was my maid of honor. Shelby, I hope you and Jackson will be as happy as Lloyd and I were. We had such a good time. Until last November…at least he hung on through the state playoffs.

SHELBY. Miss Clairee. There are still good times to be had.

CLAIREE. Oh sure. But I miss the whirlwind of being a mayor's wife. It's not easy being just one. I don't like going to things by myself.

If I go with another couple, I'm a third wheel. If I go with a friend, we're just a couple of old biddies.

SHELBY. Somebody like you should be able to find something to occupy your time.

CLAIREE. Well. I really do love football. But it's hard to parlay that into a reason to live.

TRUVY. Let's just face it, Clairee. You're a woman coming to terms with her grips. You and I are in the same boat. My kids are leaving town and I've got a husband that hasn't moved from in front of the TV set in fifteen years. It's up to us to figure out why we were put on this earth. That's today's sermon. So. Shelby. Are you and Jackson going to live in West Monroe or Monroe proper?

SHELBY. Monroe, of course. His law practice is there.

CLAIREE. You are so lucky, Shelby. Louisiana lawyers do well whether they want to or not.

SHELBY. I don't really care. Don't get me wrong. The money's real nice…but I just like the idea of growing old with somebody. My dream is to get old and sit on the back porch covered with grandchildren and say, "No!" and "Stop that!"

TRUVY. Are you going to quit nursing?

SHELBY. Never! I love it. I love being around all those babies… Last week we had this poor little fellow, two and a half months premature. He looked like a big rat. I kept talking to him and holding him. But I knew he wasn't going to make it.

TRUVY. That's so sad.

SHELBY. It happens all the time.

M'LYNN. Drum and I feel that Shelby should not work anymore after she gets married.

SHELBY. I'm so anxious to discuss this topic for the nine hundredth time this week…

M'LYNN. You should not be on your feet all day. You should be kinder to your circulatory system.

SHELBY. *(Changing subject.)* Annelle? I know you're new and all, but don't let that stop you. Anytime you have anything to say, you just let 'er rip.

ANNELLE. I don't have anything to say.

TRUVY. Well, M'Lynn. It looks like you're ready to roll. I think we can trust Annelle to roll you up, don't you? Do you think you can roll up Mrs. Eatenton, Annelle?

ANNELLE. I don't know. Today is very special. And my work tends to be too poofy when I'm nervous. Does your dress have to go over your head?

SHELBY. You can't screw up her hair. You just tease it and make it look like a blond football helmet.

M'LYNN. I must have missed the passage in *Emily Post* that said all abuse must be heaped on the mother of the bride. Go ahead, Annelle. I'm sure you'll do a beautiful job. It doesn't matter what I look like anyway.

TRUVY. Hush girls. Shelby. Tell me things about the wedding. How many bridesmaids?

SHELBY. Nine.

TRUVY. Good Lord!

SHELBY. Exactly.

TRUVY. I hope that photographer brings a wide-angle lens.

SHELBY. I think it's embarrassing and awful. But Mama made me have my cousins, and Margi St. Maurice.

M'LYNN. Shelby. There was no way around it and you know it.

SHELBY. It will be pretentious. Daddy always says, "An ounce of pretension is worth a pound of manure."

M'LYNN. The poet laureate of Dogwood Lane...

SHELBY. Mama. I wish you would get off Daddy's back. He gets enough hassle from Miss Ouiser.

TRUVY. *(The peacemaker.)* What are your colors, Shelby?

SHELBY. Blush and bashful.

M'LYNN. Her colors are pink and pink.

SHELBY. Blush and bashful.

M'LYNN. I ask you. How precious is this wedding going to get?

SHELBY. My colors are blush and bashful. I have chosen two shades of pink. One is much deeper than the other.

M'LYNN. The bridesmaids' dresses are beautiful...

SHELBY. And the ceremony will be too. All the walls are banked with sprays of flowers in the two shades of blush and bashful. There's a pink carpet specially laid for the service. And pink silk bunting draped over anything that would stand still.

M'LYNN. That sanctuary looks like it's been hosed down with Pepto-Bismol.

SHELBY. I like pink.

M'LYNN. I tried to talk her into using peaches and cream. That would be so lovely this time of year. All the azaleas in our yard are peach colored. Peach is so flattering to every skin tone.

SHELBY. No way. Pink is my signature color.

TRUVY. What color is your dress, M'Lynn?

M'LYNN. Peach and cream.

TRUVY. Clairee?

CLAIREE. Beige lace to the knee.

TRUVY. I am wearing a sexy blue chiffon, Shelby. Jackson's gonna take one look at me and leave you behind in the dust.

SHELBY. Mama's dress is gorgeous. It cost more than my wedding dress.

M'LYNN. It did not. It was on sale.

SHELBY. That's what she told Daddy. What she actually meant is that it was "for sale" not "on sale." *(The phone rings.)*

TRUVY. I'll get it. *(Answers.)* Hello. Hi, Janice. Yes, I heard. I know it's an emergency...but today I'm dealing with Shelby. But tomorrow's Sunday—but... *(Just to get off the phone.)* ...sure, fine...come by after church. *(Hangs up in disgust.)*

CLAIREE. Truvy, you shouldn't give up your Sundays.

TRUVY. Well, you know how neurotic Janice Van Meter is about her appearance.

CLAIREE. *(To Annelle.)* Janice is the current mayor's wife. *(Sweetly.)* We hate her.

TRUVY. Now Shelby...fill me in on the reception.

SHELBY. There's going to be ferns and twinkly lights. There'll be magnolias in the pool.

M'LYNN. I just hope your father doesn't get any magnolias from Ouiser's side of the tree. We'll never hear the end of it.

SHELBY. The wedding cake will be by the pool. The groom's cake will be hidden in the carport.

M'LYNN. Shelby and I agree on one thing.

SHELBY. The groom's cake. It's awful! It's in the shape of a giant armadillo.

TRUVY. An armadillo?

SHELBY. Jackson wanted a cake in the shape of an armadillo. He has an aunt that makes them.

CLAIREE. It's unusual.

M'LYNN. It's repulsive. It has gray icing. I can't even think of how you would make gray icing.

SHELBY. Worse! The cake part is red velvet cake. Blood red! People are going to be hacking into this animal that looks like it's bleeding to death.

M'LYNN. The rehearsal supper was an experience.

SHELBY. It wasn't that bad. It was out at Jackson's uncle's place on the river.

M'LYNN. They served steak and baked potatoes. They went to a lot of trouble.

SHELBY. His family loves to barbecue.

M'LYNN. For dessert they served an original creation called "Dago" pie. I think that says it all. Jackson is from a good old Southern family with good old Southern values. You either shoot it, stuff it, or marry it.

SHELBY. They are simply outdoorsy, that's all.

TRUVY. Did you all do anything especially romantic?

SHELBY. We drove down to Frenchman's Point and went parking.

M'LYNN. Shelby, really.

TRUVY. Oh, boy. The romantic part. This is what really melts my butter.

SHELBY. Then we went skinny-dipping and did things that frightened the fish.

M'LYNN. Shelby.

CLAIREE. It's been a long time since we've had a youngster in this place, hasn't it?

SHELBY. We talked, and talked, and talked...

TRUVY. I love those kinds of talks...in the arms of the man you love.

SHELBY. Actually we fought most of the time.

TRUVY. What?

SHELBY. Because I told him I couldn't marry him. *(Shock all around.)*

M'LYNN. What?

CLAIREE. Why would you go and do a thing like that?

SHELBY. It's OK now. We worked it all out.

TRUVY. Oh. It was just one of those last-minute jitter things.

SHELBY. No. But the wedding's still on.

TRUVY. Thank goodness. *(Pointing to Shelby's hairstyle.)* 'Cause this is going to be in the hairdo hall of fame.

CLAIREE. You scared us, Shelby. That wasn't a nice thing to do to your mama. You should never say something like that to a woman who's marinating fifty pounds of crab claws.

TRUVY. Oooo. Making up can be extremely romantic. I'm jealous. I miss romance so much.

CLAIREE. Truvy. It can't be that bad.

TRUVY. The last romantic thing my husband did was in 1972. He enclosed this carport so I could support him! Very nice Annelle. I think you know what you're doing.

ANNELLE. Thank you. Mrs. Eatenton, you have great hair. And your scalp's clean as a whistle.

M'LYNN. I try.

TRUVY. Must run in the family. Shelby. You have such pretty hair...so thick... *(Shelby's head is beginning to drop forward. She resists Truvy's touch.)* Hold your head up, darling.

SHELBY. Stop it.

TRUVY. Shelby? Shelby? M'Lynn!

M'LYNN. *(Upon realization, springs into action. There is no alarm, just efficient action.)* Oh honey.

CLAIREE. *(Also aware.)* I'll get some juice. *(Clairee exits into kitchen for juice.)*

M'LYNN. Truvy. There's some candy in my purse.

TRUVY. I got a peppermint right here. *(Truvy slips the candy into Shelby's mouth. Shelby spits out the candy.)*

M'LYNN. *(Attending to Shelby.)* Shelby? We're getting you some juice.

TRUVY. Should I get her a cookie?

CLAIREE. *(Returns with orange juice.)* Here's the juice.

M'LYNN. *(To Truvy.)* Shelby? You need some juice. *(Tries to get Shelby to drink.)*

SHELBY. Leave me alone.

M'LYNN. Drink, honey. Drink some juice.

TRUVY. Drink the juice, honey.

SHELBY. *(Pushing away the juice, spilling it.)* No!

CLAIREE. *(Refilling the glass.)* Who can blame her. Juice after a peppermint?

SHELBY. Mama. Stop it. I have candy in my purse.

M'LYNN. You didn't bring your purse, honey. Here. Have another sip.

SHELBY. No... *(But Shelby drinks a sip.)*

M'LYNN. It's not any wonder. With all this wedding nonsense and running around.

ANNELLE. Excuse me. Should I call the doctor or something?

TRUVY. No, no.

CLAIREE. Shelby's a diabetic.

M'LYNN. She's got a little too much insulin, that's all. She'll be fine if we can get something in her. Drink some more, Shelby.

SHELBY. I'm going to leave if you don't leave me alone.

M'LYNN. I'd love to see you try. Shelby...cooperate. Drink.

TRUVY. Honey, drink…please. *(Shelby drinks some.)*

M'LYNN. There we go. That's a start.

CLAIREE. That one hit her quick.

M'LYNN. Yes. She's on the pill now and her hormones are running wild. She'll get on an even keel pretty soon.

CLAIREE. She could hurt herself, M'Lynn? What if this happened when she was driving a car?

M'LYNN. Perhaps that explains why I have so much gray hair. But you've known Shelby as long as I have. You know I have to let her be strong. *(Shelby drinks.)* She doesn't seem to be down too deep.

CLAIREE. Talk to us, Shelby.

SHELBY. No.

CLAIREE. That's good enough.

M'LYNN. She's been so upset lately. She and Jackson have been going round and round. Dr. Michoud told her at her last appointment that children are not possible. It wasn't the easiest thing in the world to sit there and watch your child's heart break.

SHELBY. Don't talk about me like I'm not here.

M'LYNN. There. She's making some sense. This one wasn't bad at all. But I think we should have a little more juice.

ANNELLE. Can I do something? Should I…

M'LYNN. No. She'll be fine in just a minute. She probably won't remember anything. Don't fuss over her… Normality is very important to Shelby.

TRUVY. I'm sorry to hear about the children part, M'Lynn.

M'LYNN. I know. She feels that Jackson might be throwing away his chance for children. They've discussed it and he seems to have taken it alright… Shelby's the one that's pushing the issue. He's crazy about her and…

SHELBY. He said, "Shut up. Don't be stupid. There's plenty of kids out there that need good homes. We'll adopt ten of 'em. We'll buy 'em if we have to."

CLAIREE. Jackson sounds like good people to me.

SHELBY. I knew right then and there that if he was dumb enough to spend the rest of his life with me, then I'm dumb enough to marry him. *(Shelby is recovering. She realizes what has happened and is embarrassed.)* Oh gosh...oh gosh...I'm sorry...I'm so sorry, Mama. *(M'Lynn hugs Shelby. The phone rings.)*

TRUVY. *(Answering.)* Hello? Yeah, hon...just a second. M'Lynn? It's Tommy...for Shelby.

M'LYNN. Shelby, honey? It's Tommy.

TRUVY. Shelby, it's Tommy. He wants to know where your car is.

SHELBY. Absolutely not. That's the honeymoon getaway car. He just wants to defile it. Jonathan said he's been buying rubbers by the case.

TRUVY. She'll have to call you back.

SHELBY. *(To M'Lynn.)* Thank you, Mama. *(M'Lynn returns to Annelle, who continues working on her hair.)*

TRUVY. Sit up straight. I've got to gild the lily. Now. Are you going to take it down after the reception? I'll be glad to give you a touch-up before you leave on the honeymoon.

SHELBY. I'm going to leave it up as long as possible.

TRUVY. Now. Let me guess where the honeymoon is. I picture tropical. Moonlight for days. Secluded. Somewhere that you can be intimate out of doors...

SHELBY. Las Vegas.

TRUVY. The weather's supposed to be nice. I hear it's like living in a blow dryer.

M'LYNN. Shelby? About what Jackson said...

SHELBY. I'd rather not talk about it, Mama. What happens in my life now is between Jackson and me. Jackson will take care of me and I will take care of him.

CLAIREE. You can't blame people for being concerned about you, darling.

M'LYNN. What Jackson said about children...about adoption... was wonderful. And very wise. Not being able to have children is no disgrace. *(Silence.)* Shelby? Did you hear what I said?

SHELBY. Mama. I know all about adoption. And I also know the limitations of this body of mine. I would never do anything stupid.

M'LYNN. Finally. You're listening to reason.

TRUVY. Now, Shelby. You're going to have to start untangling this baby's breath.

M'LYNN. Oh, Shelby…no.

SHELBY. It's my wedding! I'll stick baby's breath up my nose if I want to.

TRUVY. She's got enough…

M'LYNN. Fine. Fine. I am supposed to be the expert on behavior and I can't seem to manage the people in my own family.

SHELBY. Oh! Did you tell them, Mama?

CLAIREE. Tell us what?

M'LYNN. Oh, it's nothing really. I might be promoted to administrator of the Mental Guidance Center.

CLAIREE. Wonderful! That Guidance Center does such good work for the disturbed.

TRUVY. I wish I'd taken my boys there when they were little and straightened them out. I should've realized Louie had problems when his imaginary playmates wouldn't play with him.

SHELBY. Your boys grew up fine. They're just a little scary that's all.

TRUVY. I just think it must be fun for M'Lynn to have access to all that secret personal information. Come on, M'Lynn. Tell us some of your most bizarre mental cases and let us guess who they are. There's a lot of sick tickets in this town.

M'LYNN. I will not discuss office business in a social setting. People need a place they can come unload their problems. I would never violate their confidence.

SHELBY. When Mama says she doesn't talk, she means it. She's a brick wall.

CLAIREE. As somebody always said…if you don't have anything nice to say about anybody…come sit by me.

M'LYNN. *(Ignoring.)* Do you realize we are being rude to poor Annette?

ANNELLE. Elle…

M'LYNN. Annelle. She doesn't know us from Adam's house cat

and we just keep talking about things foreign to her experiences. Annelle, tell us about yourself.

ANNELLE. There's nothing to tell.

M'LYNN. Where do you live?

ANNELLE. On the corner of Jefferson and Second.

M'LYNN. Which corner?

ANNELLE. The one where you can't see the house for the weeds.

M'LYNN. You must live in Mrs. Robeline's house.

ANNELLE. She's my landlady.

M'LYNN. Are you getting along with her?

ANNELLE. What's the matter with her?

M'LYNN. Nothing…nothing. Are you happy there?

ANNELLE. She scares me. She's always watching me. Sometimes I catch her looking through my keyhole.

M'LYNN. Oh. Dear me. Uh. Don't worry. She's probably not taking her medication. I'll check on her Monday. *(Beat.)* Shelby? Would you like to finish off that juice?

SHELBY. I'm fine, Mama. You finish it.

M'LYNN. Why don't you drink it? It's going to be a while before the bridesmaids' luncheon.

SHELBY. You know what you need in here, Truvy? You need a radio. Music is wonderful to have in the background. It takes the pressure off having to talk so much.

TRUVY. I used to have one, but I slammed it against the wall when I couldn't figure out where the batteries went. I know now I was the victim of premenstrual syndrome.

SHELBY. I've gotten four radios for wedding presents. I'll give you one.

TRUVY. How sweet!

CLAIREE. What did I just hear? Oh, yes. The Antilly family is selling KPPD. I wonder how much radio stations sell for?

M'LYNN. A lot. But a small-town radio station can be a license to print money if it's run right.

SHELBY. Miss Clairee. You should buy KPPD. You got plenty of money.

CLAIREE. What would I do with a radio station? Business never interested me at all. Lloyd took care of all that stuff.

M'LYNN. Shelby, why don't you finish off that juice?

SHELBY. Forget the damn juice.

M'LYNN. Shelby'll be fine now. Anyway I always carry some mints in my bag just in case.

TRUVY. Then take some of the butterscotch in that dish. Throw some in her bag, Clairee. They are the best. They start out real hard, but once you suck all the coating off, they get real chewy. My two favorite things…crunchy and chewy and buttery…all in one. Delicious. *(Clairee dumps some in M'Lynn's bag and notices something odd.)*

CLAIREE. M'Lynn. You always carry candy in your bag?

M'LYNN. Without fail.

CLAIREE. Then tell me. Do you suck on this often? *(Clairee pulls a huge gun from the bag. Gasps all around.)*

M'LYNN. Clairee. Put that back.

TRUVY. I hate it when people bring weapons into my shop.

SHELBY. How did you get Daddy's gun away from him?

M'LYNN. I had been waiting all morning for my chance. He finally put it down to go to the bathroom.

ANNELLE. I'd like to ask a question. I'm new here and all. Is my life in danger?

TRUVY. No. M'Lynn's husband's just been shooting at some birds. The trees around here are full of 'em this time of year.

M'LYNN. You see, our backyard is full of fruit trees…

SHELBY. Which are full of birds. Daddy has been trying to frighten the birds out of the trees by making loud noises. I didn't want the guests at my reception to spend all night dodging bird *do.*

M'LYNN. The neighborhood is fit to be tied. Ouiser Boudreaux blames my husband's gunshots for the problems of that mangy dog of hers. She insists all the noise has made that stupid animal lose its hair.

TRUVY. Taking the gun was a stroke of genius, M'Lynn.

M'LYNN. I know.

ANNELLE. What if he comes over here and tries to get his gun back?

M'LYNN. Drum would never set foot in a beauty shop. This is women's territory. He probably thinks we all run around naked or something.

ANNELLE. *(Catching a glimpse out of the window.)* There's somebody coming! A strange lady with a strange dog!

CLAIREE. That would be Ouiser.

ANNELLE. That is one ugly dog. What kind of dog is that?

CLAIREE. If Rhett had hair, he would be a collie.

TRUVY. Lord. Give us strength. *(The door bursts open. It's Ouiser, very upset.)*

OUISER. This is it. I've found it. I am in hell!

TRUVY. 'Morning, Ouiser.

OUISER. Don't try to get on my good side. I no longer have one.

TRUVY. You're a little early. You're not expected 'til elevenish.

OUISER. That's precisely why I'm here. I have to cancel. *(The phone rings. Ouiser picks it up and hangs up on the caller.)* I have to take my poor dog to the vet before he has a nervous breakdown. My dog I mean. The vet is perfectly healthy. *(To Annelle.)* You must be the new girl.

ANNELLE. Hi.

OUISER. May I have a glass of water? I have been screaming this morning. *(Exit Annelle.)*

M'LYNN. I'm sorry this whole thing has gotten out of hand, Ouiser...

OUISER. It's not your fault, M'Lynn. I used to think that you were crazy for marrying that man. Then I thought for a few years that you were just a glutton for punishment. Now I realize that you must be on some mission from God. I have not slept in days. I look like a dog's dinner. However, when I got up this morning, I decided I would try to rise above it. I would start anew. Whatever that man has done, I would overlook it in honor of your wedding day, Shelby. I thought I would make myself a little presentable and floss up the house in case somebody wanted to drop in…it being a big day in the neighborhood and all. So I go out to cut some fresh flowers for the living room. I go down to my magnolia tree and there is not a bloom on it!

M'LYNN. Ouiser. The judge has not decided whose tree that is exactly.

OUISER. It's mine! *(Enter Annelle with glass of water.)* Be that as it may…it would not be too much to ask for me to have one blossom to brighten my home. I am all alone except for my dog.

CLAIREE. You need something in your life besides that dumb animal…

OUISER. Put a lid on it, Clairee. I was standing there looking at my…*my* naked magnolia tree when I saw Drum across the way loading what appeared to be a cannon. I asked him what happened to all those magnolia blossoms. He said the wind probably blew them off during the night. Then I asked him how the wind managed to blow them all off into your pool. Then he fired at me! Is that rude or what?

M'LYNN. They're blanks. And Drum would never aim a gun at a lady.

OUISER. He's a real gentleman. I'll bet he takes the dishes out of the sink before he pees in it.

M'LYNN. That's uncalled for.

OUISER. All I know is my poor animal has to be sedated. He has a condition.

SHELBY. Are you sure that's true? Rhett is a very old dog.

OUISER. I am simply going on what the vet tells me.

CLAIREE. Which vet?

OUISER. Whitey Black.

CLAIREE. That's your first mistake. Whitey Black is a moron. I'm not even sure he has opposable thumbs.

SHELBY. Miss Ouiser, Daddy is not trying to drive you crazy. He's just trying to make my reception nice. His heart's in the right place.

OUISER. But he cannot do this to my dog! My dog is on his last legs! What am I going to do with the poor animal?

29

CLAIREE. *(Holding up the recipe box.)* I've got a lot of good recipes here.

OUISER. *(To Annelle.)* Darling...whatever your name is...would you look out the window and check on my dog while I smack Clairee on her smart mouth? You may not believe this, but these are the dearest friends I have in this town.

ANNELLE. His color's good. His skin is real pink.

SHELBY. I know for a fact there will be no more gunshots. So why don't you relax, Miss Ouiser? Have some coffee.

TRUVY. Ladies. This is going to work out beautifully. I'm almost through with Shelby. Annelle can shampoo Ouiser. See. Life can be wonderful.

OUISER. All right. As long as there's no more gunshots, I'll stay. *(To Annelle.)* What is your name? Did you tell me?

ANNELLE. Annelle.

OUISER. Fine. Are you new in town? I know everyone. I don't recall ever seeing you before.

ANNELLE. I just moved to town not too long ago.

OUISER. With your family?

ANNELLE. No'm. I don't have any family to speak of.

OUISER. With your husband?

ANNELLE. Uh...my husband? That's hard to say...I...uh...I don't know.

OUISER. You don't know?

ANNELLE. I'm not sure.

OUISER. I'm intrigued. Are you married or not? These are not difficult questions.

ANNELLE. Uh...we're not...he's not...I can't talk about it.

CLAIREE & TRUVY. Of course you can.

ANNELLE. I'm not sure if I'm married or not...he's gone!

OUISER. Honey. Men are the most horrible creatures.

ANNELLE. Everything is horrible. Bunkie...that's my husband. He left. We only moved here a month ago. He just vanished last week.

CLAIREE. No idea where he went?

ANNELLE. Nobody knows. He took all the money, my jewelry, the car. Most of my clothes were in the trunk.

TRUVY. There might have been foul play. Have you been to the police?

ANNELLE. No…but they've been to me. He's in big trouble with the law. Drugs or something. He never paid the rent so I got thrown out of our house and had to move in at crazy old Mrs. Robeline's. The police keep questioning me. But I don't know anything. They say my marriage may not be legal…

TRUVY. You should've said something.

ANNELLE. I was scared to. I need a job in the worst way and I didn't know if you'd hire someone who may or may not be married to someone who might be a dangerous criminal. But I swear to you that my personal tragedy will not interfere with my ability to do good hair.

TRUVY. Of course it won't…

ANNELLE. I really don't think things could get any worse.

OUISER. Of course they can.

SHELBY. You are so brave.

TRUVY. You must be made of courage.

ANNELLE. I'm totally alone. Checks are bouncing everywhere. Everything is going wrong. I keep asking myself…why me?

SHELBY. We are awful. We are all hateful, awful people. Here all we've been talking about is weddings and psychotic animals. We've been tearing you up inside, haven't we? I can't tell you how sorry I am. And you've had such a terrible time. Sometimes we don't know how lucky we are.

CLAIREE. What can we do to help?

SHELBY. I know one thing I can do. Tonight, you are going to drop by my house and have some bleeding armadillo groom's cake. It's going to be a great party.

ANNELLE. Oh, I couldn't. I still get real emotional sometimes…

SHELBY. I can't stand the thought of someone being unhappy or alone tonight. And if you feel yourself start getting sad, just watch my husband dance. It's very funny.

ANNELLE. You're all so nice.

TRUVY. We enjoy being nice to each other. There's not much else to do in this town.

ANNELLE. But I don't have anything to wear...

SHELBY. No problem. I'll bet I have something that'll do. I'll call the house. (Shelby dials the phone.)

TRUVY. Now. If you're interested, my garage apartment will be available soon. My son is living there now. Give me a day to straighten it up and sweep out the bed, then come look at it. I'm sure we can work out some arrangement with the rent.

ANNELLE. (Overcome.) Oh...

SHELBY. (On phone.) Good! Jonathan. You have to do me a favor. Yes, now! Go in my closet and bring me two or three of my Sunday things. Just anything. Use your judgement. Very well. Bring the pink dress with the white collar, the pink suit with the cherries pinned on the jacket and the pink and white polka dot. No, Jonathan. Mama doesn't have Daddy's gun. Don't you have better things to do? What? Well stop him! Now! (She hangs up. She is nervous.)

CLAIREE. Is something the matter?

SHELBY. We'll see. (There is a huge explosion.) Yes.

OUISER. What in the hell!!! (They all go to the window. The dog begins to bark uncontrollably.)

M'LYNN. What happened?

SHELBY. Daddy tied explosives to Jonathan's GI Joe bow and arrow and shot them into the trees.

OUISER. Shut up Rhett!

M'LYNN. I hope nobody was hurt!

TRUVY. Well, the birds are flying every which-a-way. And there's white smoke billowing up from your backyard.

CLAIREE. Looks like Drum has set his trees on fire or he's just elected a new pope.

32

ANNELLE. I guess it worked. All the birds are leaving. *(They all come away from the window except Annelle.)*

OUISER. This is all she wrote. I am going to let that man have it.

ANNELLE. *(Still at window.)* Oh no! Your dog broke his chain! And he's heading toward the smoke!

M'LYNN. Oh, no! That dog will eat Drum alive. And Drum is unarmed!

CLAIREE. Ouiser! Do something!

TRUVY. Ouiser! Call your dog! He'll listen to you!

SHELBY. Miss Ouiser! Please! It's my wedding day. Say something to your dog!

OUISER. *(Flings open the door and screams:)* Kill, Rhett! Kill! *(Everyone rushes out the door.)*

CURTAIN.

SCENE II

It is later in the year. The Saturday before Christmas, to be exact. Not much in the shop has changed. Only half of the lights are on in the shop. When the lights eventually come back on, we see the subtle changes. The radio Shelby has given Truvy, a small but festive Christmas tree, and several grotesque handicrafts. At curtain, M'Lynn is sitting under a dead hairdryer. Shelby enters, mystified by the lack of light and the lack of activity.

M'LYNN. Shelby!

SHELBY. Mama? Where is everybody?

M'LYNN. I thought you weren't coming to town until after lunch.

SHELBY. We got an early start because of the traffic. We wanted to drop in on Jackson's parents on the way down here.

M'LYNN. What a treat!

SHELBY. And you have to catch them early. On Saturdays they leave the house at the crack of dawn to start hunting furry little creatures.

M'LYNN. You must not have visited long.

SHELBY. We didn't. I could tell they were anxious to start killing things. We stopped by the house first. Nobody was there. Where's Truvy?

M'LYNN. She and Annelle are out back sticking pennies in the fuse box. They decorated that little tree and when I plugged it in all the lights blew.

SHELBY. *(Pointing to a pair of tacky earrings.)* What are those things?

M'LYNN. Red plastic poinsettia earrings. They are a gift from Annelle. She has discovered the wonderful world of Arts and Crafts.

SHELBY. Are Tommy and Jonathan home yet?

M'LYNN. Yes. Jonathan got home yesterday morning. He loves his classes. It's all he can talk about. I think the main thing architecture school has taught him is how much he should hate his parents' house. Tommy arrived last night and immediately started terrorizing your father. It's nice having the family home for Christmas.

SHELBY. Some things never change.

M'LYNN. And how are you, honey?

SHELBY. I'm so good, Mama. Just great.

M'LYNN. You're looking well. Is Jackson at the house?

SHELBY. No. You know how twitchy he gets. I sent him to look for stocking stuffers.

M'LYNN. Good thinking.

SHELBY. Uh. Jackson and I have something to tell you. We wanted to tell you when you and Daddy were together, but you're never together, so it's every man for himself. I'm pregnant.

M'LYNN. Shelby?!

SHELBY. I'm going to have a baby.

M'LYNN. I realize that.

34

SHELBY. Well…is that it? Is that all you're going to say?

M'LYNN. I…what do you expect me to say?

SHELBY. Something along the lines of congratulations.

M'LYNN. …Congratulations.

SHELBY. Would it be too much to ask for a little excitement? Not too much, I wouldn't want you to break a sweat or anything.

M'LYNN. I'm in a state of shock! I didn't think…

SHELBY. In June. Oh, Mama. You have to help me plan. We're going to get a new house. Jackson and I are going house hunting next week. Jackson loves to hunt for anything.

M'LYNN. What does Jackson say about this?

SHELBY. Oh. He's very excited. He says he doesn't care whether it's a boy or girl…but I know he really wants a son so bad he can taste it. He's so cute about the whole thing. It's all he can talk about… Jackson Latcherie Junior.

M'LYNN. But does he ever listen? I mean when doctors and specialists give you advice. I know you never listen, but does he? I guess since he doesn't have to carry the baby, it doesn't really concern him.

SHELBY. Mama. Don't be mad. I couldn't bear it if you were. It's Christmas.

M'LYNN. I'm not mad, Shelby. This is just…hard. I thought that… I don't know.

SHELBY. Mama. I want a child.

M'LYNN. But what about the adoption proceedings? You have filed so many applications.

SHELBY. Mama. It didn't take us long to see the handwriting on the wall. No judge is going to give a baby to someone with my medical track record. Jackson even put out some feelers about buying one.

M'LYNN. People do it all the time.

SHELBY. Listen to me. I want a child of my own. I think it would help things a lot.

M'LYNN. I see.

SHELBY. Mama. I know. I know. Don't think I haven't thought this through. You can't live a life if all you do is worry. And you worry too much. In some ways it's a comfort to me. I never worry because I know you're worrying enough for the both of us. Jackson and I have given this a lot of thought.

M'LYNN. Has he really? There's a first time for everything.

SHELBY. Don't start on Jackson.

M'LYNN. Shelby. Your poor body has been through so much. Why do you deliberately want to…

SHELBY. Mama. Diabetics have healthy babies all the time.

M'LYNN. You are special. There are limits to what you can do.

SHELBY. Mama…listen. I have it all planned. I'm going to be very careful. And this time next year, I'm going to be bringing your big healthy grandbaby to the Christmas festival. No one is going to be hurt or disappointed, or even inconvenienced.

M'LYNN. Least of all Jackson, I'm sure.

SHELBY. You are jealous because you no longer have any say-so in what I do. And that drives you up the wall. You're ready to spit nails because you can't call the shots.

M'LYNN. I did not raise my daughter to talk to me this way.

SHELBY. Yes you did. Whenever any of us asked you what you wanted us to be when we grew up, what did you say?

M'LYNN. Shelby, I am not in the mood for games.

SHELBY. What did you say? Just tell me what you said. Answer me.

M'LYNN. I said all I wanted was for you to be happy.

SHELBY. OK. The thing that would make me happy is to have a baby. If I could adopt one I would, but I can't. I'm going to have a baby. I wish you would be happy, too.

M'LYNN. I wish I… I don't know what I wish.

SHELBY. Mama. I don't know why you have to make everything so difficult. I look at having this baby as the opportunity of a lifetime. Sure, there may be some risk involved. That's true for anybody. But you get through it and life goes on. And when it's all said and done there'll be a little piece of immortality with Jackson's looks and my sense of style…I hope. Mama, please. I need your support. I would rather have thirty minutes of wonderful than a lifetime of nothing special. *(The lights come up. The radio is blaring.)*

M'LYNN. They're on, Truvy!

SHELBY. Please. Don't tell anybody yet. I want to tell Daddy first.

M'LYNN. I never tell anyone anything. *(M'Lynn goes to turn the radio volume down.)*

TRUVY. *(Enters, carrying Christmas decorations.)* Well! Look who's here! Give me a hug right here and now!

SHELBY. Hi, Truvy! Merry Christmas!

TRUVY. Ho, ho, ho. *(Calling through the door.)* Annelle! We have a special mystery guest! *(To Shelby.)* You're just in time. You can have the honor of lighting the tree of beauty.

SHELBY. How precious. What a novel idea to trim it with hair things.

TRUVY. *(Annelle enters.)* It's all Annelle's idea. She has quite an eye for the unusual.

ANNELLE. Hi there! *(Hugs Shelby.)*

SHELBY. *(The tree and the decorations.)* Annelle, you did all this?

ANNELLE. Guilty. Truvy just turned over the decoration responsibility to me. I like themes. And I despise the commercialization of Christmas, always have. So I went to the fire sale at the Baptist Book Store in Shreveport last month. They had mismatched Manger scenes at incredibly low prices. I cleaned them out of Baby Jesuses, which Truvy's husband helped me modify into ornaments. Very simple. Tiny white lights, Baby Jesuses, and spoolies.

TRUVY. My husband has redone Poot's old room so Annelle can have a workshop for her handicrafts. That little garage apartment is so cramped. *(Truvy places grotesque handmade treetop ornament on tree.)*

SHELBY. Isn't that nice. Are your boys coming home for Christmas?

TRUVY. No. Louie brought home his girlfriend at Thanksgiving. The nicest thing I can say about her is that all her tattoos are spelled correctly. Guess it's just me, the old man…and Annelle. *(Offers Shelby the plug for the lights.)* Do the honors, missy. And hope it doesn't blow up again. *(Shelby lights the tree. Applause all around.)*

SHELBY. *(Triumphantly to M'Lynn.)* See. I know what I'm doing.

TRUVY. I know your mother is so happy you could get in early enough to make the festival. I hear it's going to be the best ever. More fireworks, a nativity made entirely of sparklers, and a huge new sign on the riverbank that says, "I Heart Chinquapin Parish." It's going to be spectacular. And guess who the grand marshal of the parade is? Wayne Newton!

SHELBY. I wouldn't miss a Christmas festival for the world. *(Truvy and Annelle begin decorating. Shelby gets M'Lynn's attention from under the dryer.)* Oh. Mama. While I'm thinking. I brought some white chocolate cherry cheesecakes for our open house.

M'LYNN. That doesn't sound like finger food to me.

SHELBY. They're bite-sized. Like this.

M'LYNN. Fine. I'm sure you know what you're doing.

TRUVY. *(Seeking Annelle's approval on decoration placement.)* Annelle?

ANNELLE. Perfect.

SHELBY. And, Mama? I've been cleaning out closets…getting rid of stuff. I've brought you some things I don't want that I've hardly worn. I thought maybe your patients might be less disturbed if they had something stylish to wear.

TRUVY. *(Wondering where to put some decorations.)* Annelle?

ANNELLE. The chair. *(To Shelby.)* Uh. Excuse me, Shelby? Uh. If you don't have any special plans for the clothes…could I have them? Riverview Baptist has a clothes closet for the poor. We're real low on women's dresses.

SHELBY. Sure. That's a wonderful idea. They're in the car. I'll get 'em in a minute.

TRUVY. It breaks my heart that she won't come to the Methodist church with me. I think Riverview Baptist is a little too…"Praise the Lord" for my taste.

ANNELLE. *(With an edge.)* Some of them do get a little carried away. But there's nothing wrong with that.

SHELBY. No. A lot of Mama's mental patients are born-again Christians. I mean that only in the best sense of the word.

TRUVY. We're just glad to see that Annelle is settling down and finding her way. She's had a few rough months, haven't you, honey?

38

ANNELLE. Oh. After they finally threw Bunkie Dupuy behind bars and I was rid of him, I went wild. I was drinking, running around, smoking…

TRUVY. Jezebel!

ANNELLE. But Truvy helped me see the error of my ways. I've realized I have something to offer. I joined a church last month. Truvy's helped me see I have talents. I've done guest lectures on beauty at the trade school…

TRUVY. Our little Annelle has become one of the hottest tickets in town.

ANNELLE. Truvy. Stop. I am enjoying the city more. And I am so excited about the Christmas festival today. I've wanted to come to it all my life. And now I live here!

TRUVY. Tell her who you have a date with.

ANNELLE. Truvy, will you hush?

TRUVY. Tell her, missy. Shelby is pretty much totally responsible for the whole thing!

ANNELLE. Sammy DeSoto.

TRUVY. He has a body that doesn't stop anywhere.

SHELBY. How am I responsible?

ANNELLE. He was bartending at your wedding reception last spring. That's when I met him. He makes a mean Cherry Coke.

TRUVY. Romance. This is what I live for. Can we do anything for you today, Shelby?

SHELBY. I'm beyond help. Last week I discovered the early stages of crow's feet.

TRUVY. Oh, honey. Time marches on. And eventually you realize it's marching across your face. How are you feeling?

SHELBY. Never better. *(Clairee enters. She has on a Devils cap. She is hoarse.)*

CLAIREE. *(Presenting a tin of cookies.)* My annual pecan tassies!

TRUVY. There's my girl. I guess you're the happy one this morning.

CLAIREE. Yes, I am. First state championship in eight years!

SHELBY. You sound awful, Miss Clairee!

CLAIREE. Hello, darling!

SHELBY. Can I get you some tea?

CLAIREE. Yes, that would be nice. I'm sorry I'm late. I overslept. We didn't get back into town until one o'clock. It was a dazzling victory over Dry Prong.

ANNELLE. I heard you on the radio last night. You were wonderful.

SHELBY. What were you doing on the radio?

CLAIREE. They let me be the color announcer for the Devils. I was fabulous. I was too colorful for words.

SHELBY. That was nice of them to let you talk on the radio.

CLAIREE. Nice nothing. I own the radio station.

SHELBY. Oh! You bought it?

CLAIREE. Yes!! KPPD. The station of choice in Chinquapin Parish!

TRUVY. Shelby? How do you like Clairee's new short and sassy look?

SHELBY. I love it.

TRUVY. Just wait 'til I jack it up.

SHELBY. It makes you look younger, Miss Clairee.

CLAIREE. My hair looks younger. My face looks just as old.

ANNELLE. There is so much going on! The state championship last night, the Christmas festival today, the Messiah sing-along tomorrow...

TRUVY. Life in the big city will spoil you.

SHELBY. Who's Miss Merry Christmas this year?

CLAIREE. My niece, Nancy Beth, of course.

TRUVY. She was here at seven this morning. I had to position her tiara properly on her head so it wouldn't slip around during the parade. I sprayed her hair within an inch of its life.

SHELBY. Why did I have to ask? I should have known. All you Marmillions are gorgeous. Beauty is genetic in your family.

CLAIREE. Nancy Beth is a pretty girl. Do you know she is Miss Merry Christmas, Miss Soybean, and Miss Watermelon?

TRUVY. But dumb as a post.

CLAIREE. Empty is the head that wears the crown.

TRUVY. You have to admit God did a little dance around that family. Drew is so successful. Belle does her own hair. Their children are perfect. They're like a family on TV. They don't have a care in the world.

M'LYNN. That's not necessarily true.

TRUVY. Oh?

M'LYNN. That's all I'm saying.

TRUVY. Oh.

SHELBY. I should've won Miss Merry Christmas the year I ran. My talent was very showy.

CLAIREE. We told you at the time, Shelby. Fire batons are not everyone's cup of tea.

SHELBY. Mama didn't approve of my twirling fire batons.

M'LYNN. I just don't approve when you insist on doing dangerous things.

SHELBY. Mama hated those fire batons.

M'LYNN. I have never hated anything, Shelby. I supported you, but I just couldn't watch you. Your father, on the other hand, had a field day. He got so much pleasure out of standing in the backyard for hours watching you practice, holding the garden hose so he could put you out when you caught fire.

SHELBY. My entire pageant ensemble was coordinated in shades of pink...soup to nuts. I twirled to the music from *Hawaii 5-0*. It was my theme song.

M'LYNN. But we were proud of her.

TRUVY. The year I competed, the swimsuit competition was my downfall. Most women look for a swimsuit that will lift and separate; I look for one that will divide and conquer. I've always been built for comfort, not for speed.

SHELBY. Who got the title your year, Miss Clairee?

CLAIREE. Oh, child. Nobody. There wasn't even a Christmas festival when I was in high school. Why Jesus wasn't even born until I was a junior in college. I remember it distinctly. My friends and I were all out watching our flocks by night...

TRUVY. Get over here, Clairee. Annelle's gotta gift wrap your head.

OUISER. *(Entering in a huff.)* I could just spit.

TRUVY. 'Morning Ouiser.

OUISER. The parade doesn't even start for four hours and already people are parking on my lawn. It will flatten my grass.

CLAIREE. *(Mock sincerity.)* Here. Let me hold you.

OUISER. I hate out-of-town tourists.

SHELBY. Hello!

OUISER. Shelby! What are you doing here?

SHELBY. Being a tourist, I guess. But I won't flatten your grass, I promise.

OUISER. Good God. You've had the good sense to move away from this festival madness. I can't understand why you'd drag yourself back for a couple of firecrackers and drunk teenagers earping on your shoes.

SHELBY. I like it.

ANNELLE. Miss Ouiser. I think you need a healthy dose of Christmas spirit. *(Annelle interrupts conditioning Clairee to get a present from the tree.)*

OUISER. I have so much Christmas spirit I could scream.

ANNELLE. *(Handing her a present.)* Merry Christmas!

OUISER. *(Opening present.)* I just finished putting out my yard decorations.

CLAIREE. Ouiser. Keep off the grass signs are not Christmas decorations.

OUISER. They are bordered in holly. *(Pulls out poinsettia earrings.)* You made them, didn't you?

ANNELLE. With my own two hands.

OUISER. Your present is...uh...back at the house. I haven't wrapped it yet.

SHELBY. How's Rhett?

OUISER. He's getting along. As a matter of fact, he's the poster dog for the Christmas festival. *(Ouiser points to a poster on the wall with a picture on it.)*

TRUVY. That is Rhett! I didn't recognize him.

CLAIREE. It's nice to see Rhett with some hair again.

SHELBY. I have to run some errands, but before I go...Miss Ouiser. I have met an old friend of yours.

OUISER. Oh?

SHELBY. Owen Jenkins.

OUISER. Oh.

CLAIREE. Owen? Now there's a blast from the past.

SHELBY. Do you remember him? He remembers you.

OUISER. Of course I remember him. He had the longest nose hair in the free world.

SHELBY. He doesn't now. He hardly has any hair anywhere.

CLAIREE. Owen's been gone from Chinquapin since God was a boy. I'd forgotten he'd ever existed.

SHELBY. Well now Owen lives in Monroe and goes to First Presbyterian. He sings in the choir. One night at choir practice we were doing an especially beautiful Mozart thing and I was moved to tears. He offered me his handkerchief and we got to talking. When he found out where I was from he asked me if I knew you. I said not only did I know you, but you were a neighbor and your dog has almost killed my father on numerous occasions. He's had a very interesting life. He lived in Ohio somewhere. His wife just died recently and he moved back down here.

OUISER. Does this story have a point?

SHELBY. No, not really. He just remembers you fondly, I think.

OUISER. Can't imagine why. He wasn't a bad fellow. But I managed to run him off and marry the first of two total deadbeats.

TRUVY. Unrequited love. My favorite.

SHELBY. Maybe sometime I could arrange for us all to get together.

OUISER. Maybe not.

SHELBY. Why not?

OUISER. Shelby. I managed in just a few decades to marry the two most worthless men in the universe and proceed to have the three most ungrateful children ever conceived. The only reason people are nice to me is because I have more money than God. I am not about to open a new can of worms.

CLAIREE. Do I detect a negativity in your tone?

M'LYNN. If this is really the way you feel, Ouiser, it isn't healthy. Maybe you should think about coming down and talking to someone at the Guidance Center. We're there to help.

OUISER. I'm not crazy. I've just been in a very bad mood for forty years.

SHELBY. Well. Annelle? What do you want me to do with these old clothes? I need to get them out of the back seat.

ANNELLE. Just bring 'em in.

SHELBY. OK. Then I'll go finish my Christmas shopping, Mama.

TRUVY. I could shoot you. I haven't even started.

CLAIREE. Please. I haven't even washed the dishes from Thanksgiving.

ANNELLE. What did you get your mama?

SHELBY. I told her this morning what part of it was.

TRUVY. Well, let's hear it, missy.

M'LYNN. I think it's a secret.

OUISER. Obviously there's no such thing in this room.

M'LYNN. It's up to you, honey.

SHELBY. I'm going to have a baby. *(Whoops and joy all around. Except for M'Lynn.)*

TRUVY. Congratulations! No wonder you haven't said much this morning, M'Lynn. *(Taunts.)* Grandma! Aren't you excited? Smile! It increases your face value!

SHELBY. June 21.

TRUVY. And those doctors said you couldn't have children. What do they know? I guess you showed them.

M'LYNN. The doctor said Shelby *shouldn't* have children. There's a big difference. I guess you showed us all, Shelby.

SHELBY. I've got to get the clothes. Miss Ouiser? Are you bringing your shrimp meat pies to our open house tonight?

OUISER. Don't I always? They'll be there.

44

SHELBY. Good. So will Owen Jenkins. I opened the worms for you. *(Shelby exits.)*

OUISER. I can't believe she did that. Owen? After all these years? I'm not sure I can be gracious under pressure.

M'LYNN. Shelby, Shelby. Her heart does get the best of her sometimes.

TRUVY. This baby. That's not exactly great news, is it?

M'LYNN. She wants this so badly. I just don't know...

CLAIREE. Oh boy...

TRUVY. Oh, honey. I wish I had some words of wisdom...but I don't. So I will focus on the joy of the situation. Congratulations.

OUISER. Absolutely.

M'LYNN. Diabetics have healthy babies all the time.

ANNELLE. It will all be fine.

CLAIREE. Of course it will.

M'LYNN. Thank you, ladies. You're right. We'll make it through this just fine. You know what they say. That which does not kill us makes us stronger.

OUISER. *(Looking out window.)* What is that girl up to?

ANNELLE. Shelby's donating some clothes to the poor.

OUISER. *(Opening door for Shelby.)* I hope poor people like pink.

TRUVY. *(To Shelby.)* Just dump 'em on the couch.

ANNELLE. Miss M'Lynn, you sure you don't mind me taking them? If your patients need them...

M'LYNN. No, no. Shelby said you could have 'em. And what she says goes.

SHELBY. That's not true, Mama.

M'LYNN. Shelby, you always insist on having the last word.

SHELBY. *(At the door.)* I do not. *(She slams the door and runs off. Lights out and the bombastic sounds of Handel's* Messiah *fill the air as we have...)*

CURTAIN.

ACT TWO

In the blackout before curtain, we hear the radio. It is a male DJ for KPPD. Totally fatuous and self-possessed, it is his voice we hear over the radio throughout Act Two.

DJ. You're listening to KPPD, the station of choice in Chinquapin Parish. Now stop by the shopping center this afternoon. I'll be broadcasting al fresco...that means out of doors for those of you that aren't Latin scholars. There'll be prizes, and a battle of the bands, all sponsored by KPPD. Swing on by and meet me in person. See how good-looking I really am. Coming up now...a half hour of nonstop music so I can make it over to the shopping center. Let's hope none of these records has a scratch on 'em, 'cause I'm outta here. I'm gonna kick things off with one of my personal all-time favorites. *(Song starts to play.)* See ya at the shopping center!

SCENE I

It is June, eighteen months later. The radio is playing. Nothing much in the shop has changed. Maybe new curtains and a Mr. Coffee. Truvy is cutting Shelby's hair. The hair is very short, very boyish. There is an underlying uneasiness in Shelby's behavior. Clairee is being "done" by Annelle. Shelby's radio plays, but fades in and out. Truvy and Annelle have to whack it from time to time to make it play. Clairee has been regaling them with a story and they are laughing.

SHELBY. But didn't he scare you to death coming by so late?

CLAIREE. It wasn't that late. About 9:30, I guess.

SHELBY. Still, somebody knocking on my bedroom window after dark would scare the daylights out of me.

46

CLAIREE. Not me. Hope springs eternal, I suppose. I was so disappointed when I realized it was only my nephew.

SHELBY. Well I just think it's awful of Drew to throw his son out of the house. Parents should never throw their children out of the house.

CLAIREE. My brother can be very hotheaded when he wants to be. But he really didn't throw Marshall out. Marshall just came over to my house while his daddy cooled off. I adore Marshall. We stayed up half the night talking last night.

TRUVY. *(Finishing Shelby's hair with a flourish.)* Well. That's it. Are you ready to see the new Shelby Latcherie?

SHELBY. I...don't know.

TRUVY. You're gonna have to sooner or later. Our world is full of reflective surfaces.

SHELBY. I can't believe I'm getting so worked up over something as silly as a haircut.

CLAIREE. You look precious.

SHELBY. OK. I'm ready. *(Truvy turns Shelby into the mirror.)* Oh, gosh...it's so weird...

TRUVY. *(Referring to a magazine picture.)* I did what you wanted, didn't I, honey?

SHELBY. Yes. I didn't mean...of course. You did a beautiful job. I've never had short hair, that's all.

TRUVY. Well this is what we *Cosmo* girls call a "rite du passage." *(Shelby is visibly upset.)*

SHELBY. I'm sorry. I'm being so ridiculous.

TRUVY. It's OK, honey. Please don't...please don't cry because you know...I will, too. I have a strict policy that no one cries alone in my presence.

CLAIREE. Ladies...ladies. Please. *(Clairee and Annelle hand them Kleenex.)* Remind me never to take these two to see *Dark Victory*. They'd never survive.

SHELBY. *(Rallying.)* Enough! I love my hair!

TRUVY. Whew! My artistic nature is so relieved.

ANNELLE. It's very becoming. I guess with that baby, you don't have time to spend hours fussing with your hair. You need something you can just run your fingers through and go.

CLAIREE. It's totally adorable. Your mother's going to love it.

SHELBY. Mama's going to freak out. She just thinks I'm getting a trim. I wasn't up to a big debate with her this morning. Now! Truvy! Let's do my nails!

TRUVY. This *is* a treat! No one around here ever wants a manicure. I don't even know what to charge for a full day of beauty.

SHELBY. I want the works. I want to feel completely pampered today. Mama's gonna want a manicure, too.

TRUVY. I am going to paint my front door red and change my name to Elizabeth Arden.

CLAIREE. Manicures, saucy new hairdos. What's going on?

SHELBY. We're always up to something…you know that. *(Changing subject.)* But I want to get back to this Drew and Belle nonsense. I hope they reconcile with Marshall. Speaking as a parent, they better get their act together. I do not approve of friction between parents and children.

CLAIREE. Oh, I think it'll all blow over. I have to admit. He did go about it the wrong way.

TRUVY. What did he do?

CLAIREE. He marched in unexpected from Los Angeles while Drew and Belle were preparing for the annual Marmillion shrimp boil. Marshall without so much as a hello says, "Mama and Daddy. I have something to tell you. I have a brain tumor. I have three months to live." Well, naturally Drew and Belle became hysterical. Then Marshall says, "Hey folks, I'm just kidding. I'm only gay."

SHELBY. That was his idea of breaking the news gently?

CLAIREE. Drew became incredibly distraught and started throwing wet shrimp at him, screaming at him to get out of his sight, so Marshall came to my house, smelling like a can of cat food.

TRUVY. What do you think Drew and Belle are feeling right now?

CLAIREE. I don't know. They just considered themselves to be a model family for so long. First with Nancy Beth dethroned from her Miss Merry Christmas title after that unfortunate motel thing…

SHELBY. What motel thing? I don't live here anymore, remember?

TRUVY. Nancy Beth was discovered in a nearby motel with a high political official.

CLAIREE. They were both high. They'd been smoking everything but their shoes.

TRUVY. To be the only Miss Merry Christmas in history caught with her tinsel down around her knees was a very humiliating experience for the Marmillion family.

SHELBY. How do you feel about Marshall?

CLAIREE. Haven't really thought about it. But I want you to know he's always welcome at my house. I'm very proud of him. He built up that chain of sportswear stores all by himself without a penny of family money. He says, "I am a self-made man. I pulled myself up by my own jockstraps."

TRUVY. He could always turn a phrase. *(Truvy is about to use a bottle of something for Shelby's manicure, but she realizes the bottle is empty. She turns to ask Annelle for some, but Annelle is in silent prayer. Uncomfortable, Truvy waits for Annelle to finish. The others also notice Annelle.)*

ANNELLE. Amen.

TRUVY. Amen. Annelle? I'm out of uh… *(Holds up the bottle.)*

ANNELLE. Is it still next to…?

TRUVY. No. It's over the…

ANNELLE. OK. *(Annelle exits.)*

SHELBY. Was she praying?

TRUVY. Yes.

SHELBY. Why?

TRUVY. Got me. Maybe she was praying for Marshall and Drew and Belle. Maybe she was praying for us because we were gossiping. Maybe she was praying because the elastic is shot in her pantyhose. Who knows? She prays at the drop of a hat these days.

SHELBY. How long has she been this way?

TRUVY. Ever since Mardi Gras. She had her choice of going to a Bible weekend with her Sunday School class or to New Orleans with me and two other sinners. She left that Friday a pleasant, well-adjusted young lady and she returned on Tuesday a Christian.

SHELBY. What does her boyfriend say?

TRUVY. Sammy's so confused he doesn't know whether to scratch his watch or wind his butt. He's crazy about her. He says he could deal with another man in her life, but he has trouble with the father, the son, and the Holy Ghost.

SHELBY. Well, I'm pretty religious, but that stuff makes me feel kind of creepy.

TRUVY. Well, I'm torn. I've got two sons that I'm afraid are going to hell in a handcart and a semi-daughter that strives to be the kind of girl Jesus would bring home to Mama. I don't know what to think. I don't understand those people...but they sometimes seem to have a peace about things that I've never had. Maybe I'm just jealous. (Annelle enters, smacks the radio to make it play. Clairee changes subject.)

CLAIREE. And Marshall is so thoughtful. He brought me this pin. (Clairee reveals a piece of jewelry under her beauty smock.) It's gold and enamel.

TRUVY. It's a bug.

CLAIREE. It's fine jewelry. Its little eyes are rubies, my birthstone.

SHELBY. Does Marshall have a...uh...you know...friends?

CLAIREE. We talked a little bit about that. I'm such a nosy old thing. I asked him how he...met people. 'Cause in my day you could tell by a man's carriage and demeanor which side his bread was buttered on. But today? In this day and age? Who knows? I asked Marshall, "How can you tell?" and he said, "All gay men have track lighting. And all gay men are named Mark, Rick, or Steve." He is such a nut...track lighting. (Everyone laughs.)

OUISER. (Enters carrying a sack.) 'Morning.

TRUVY. 'Morning, Ouiser!

OUISER. What's so funny?

SHELBY. Miss Clairee was just telling us the true story of track lighting.

OUISER. I love mine. It highlights my new artwork.

CLAIREE. Since when do you have track lighting?

OUISER. About three weeks. It's in my foyer and up the stairs. It was my grandson's idea.

SHELBY. I haven't seen him in ages. How is he?

OUISER. Steve's fine. I brought you all some tomatoes. First of the season. I didn't expect to see you in town, Shelby.

SHELBY. Well, I'm here.

OUISER. Take some tomatoes back home with you. There's plenty. Boy! Your hair's short. Looks good!

SHELBY. Thank you, Miss Ouiser. Jack Jr. loves tomatoes…he smears them on the cafe curtains in the kitchen.

TRUVY. Your mama says you have become an incredible gourmet cook.

SHELBY. I try. When we first married all Jackson wanted was meat and potatoes and vegetables just the way his mama made them… cooked to mush. But I've broken him of that. I even got some pâté down him last week. He swore it was dog food. Jack Jr. loved it, though.

OUISER. Clairee. How many tomatoes do you want? Tomatoes have no calories and are full of… *(She throws away a wormy rotten one.)* …things.

CLAIREE. Ouiser, you're almost chipper today. Why are you in such a good mood? Did you run over a small child or something?

OUISER. Do you or do you not want tomatoes?

CLAIREE. Don't give me all of 'em.

OUISER. Somebody's got to take them. I hate 'em. I try not to eat healthy food if I can help it. The sooner this body wears out the better off I'll be. I have trouble getting enough grease into my diet.

ANNELLE. Then why do you grow them?

OUISER. I am an old Southern woman. We're supposed to put on funny-looking hats and ugly old dresses and grow vegetables in the dirt. Don't ask me why. I don't make the rules.

CLAIREE. You should get some gloves. Your hands look like a couple of T-bone steaks.

SHELBY. Health is the most important thing, Miss Ouiser. Trust me on this.

OUISER. And. While I have everyone's attention. This morning I went to my mailbox and found that someone... *(Directed at Annelle.)* has put me on the mailing list for the Riverview Baptist Church. Lucky me. I am now receiving chain letters for Christ.

ANNELLE. They aren't chain letters. They're part of my prayer group's "Reach out and touch" project. We were each supposed to write somebody in the community that we thought might be in spiritual trouble and invite them to worship. *(Ouiser plops down a big wad of mail.)* I guess you made everybody's list.

OUISER. I think it is in the worst possible taste to pray for perfect strangers.

CLAIREE. "Reach out" to Ouiser and you'll pull back a bloody stump. Shelby! I just realized! You've saved me a phone call. Next Friday Sis Orelle and I are driving up to Monroe and we'd like to take you and Jackson to dinner if we may.

SHELBY. Uh...I can't Friday night. I'm sorry. What's the occasion?

CLAIREE. This is going to sound a little silly, but we're coming up to go to the Little Theatre. We have tickets to a play.

TRUVY. I didn't know you went to see anything that didn't have a goalpost at either end.

CLAIREE. Up to now, I haven't. But Sis and I decided at bridge one day that we needed to keep up. We wanted to expose ourselves to a little more culture. And that's not easy to come by in this neck of the woods.

TRUVY. Exactly what are you "exposing" yourself to?

CLAIREE. I don't know. Something. The last thing we saw there was pretty good. It was Shakespeare. I was a little apprehensive at first, but you know what? When you get right down to it...he writes pretty straightforward stuff. I have to admit when they hide behind curtains and put little masks over their faces to fool people...that got kind of silly. Sis fell for it, but I didn't.

OUISER. Sis Orelle is so dumb. She thinks Sherlock Holmes is a subdivision.

CLAIREE. Anyway. Sis and I like it so much, we're planning a theatre trip to New York.

TRUVY. New York?! Oh, Clairee. I'm green with envy. Promise me you'll go to the first floor of Bloomingdale's and come back and tell me everything. *Woman's Day* says it's impossible to walk through there and not get made up.

CLAIREE. We're just talking. I'm scared to death of getting on a plane.

TRUVY. It's a piece of cake. You're safer flying than you are in a car. Just sit in the rear. That's the best place to survive the crash.

SHELBY. Miss Ouiser. Why don't you go to Monroe with Miss Clairee?

OUISER. I am not exposing myself to anything.

CLAIREE. You should broaden your horizons.

OUISER. You broaden your horizons your way. I'll broaden my horizons mine. I have plans next Friday. I'm going to Shreveport to have my colors done.

CLAIREE. Your what?

OUISER. I'm going to get my colors done. I'm going to find out if I'm a summer or spring or fall or winter. It's a present from Owen.

CLAIREE. What are you talking about?

OUISER. Every person has a particular coloring...summer, spring, so on. You determine what season you are, then you know what colors look best on you. Then you're given samples of the colors that are in your palette. It's most helpful when you shop for clothes. It gives you fashion courage.

CLAIREE. That is the stupidest thing I have ever heard of.

OUISER. It's all the rage.

SHELBY. A lot of my friends in Monroe have had it done.

TRUVY. There's a quiz on that very topic in that *Family Circle* right over there. I am the epitome of winter.

OUISER. Why don't you have it done, Shelby? You're so fashion-conscious.

SHELBY. No. I'm scared to. I might find out that pink is not in my palette and I'm not sure I could live with that.

CLAIREE. I have heard it all. Well. I am going to the theatre. I am going to support the arts in our area.

OUISER. I'll write a check. I will support art. I just don't want to see it.

CLAIREE. It wouldn't harelip you, you know.

OUISER. Let's get one thing straight. I don't see plays because I can nap at home for free. I don't see movies because they're all trash and full of naked people. And I don't read books because if they're any good, they'll be made into a miniseries.

SHELBY. I'm surprised you and Daddy don't get along any better than you do. Miss Ouiser? How're things with Owen? I try to check up on you, but I haven't been able to lately.

OUISER. They're alright. I enjoy his company…on occasion.

CLAIREE. I can report that the Sherwood Florist delivery truck stops by her house at least twice a week.

OUISER. He knows I like fresh flowers.

CLAIREE. And I can report that a strange car is parked in her garage at least once a week.

OUISER. There. My secret's out. I'm having an affair with a Mercedes-Benz.

TRUVY. Ouiser. Forgive me. I have been dying to ask this. Are you and Owen…you know?

CLAIREE. Wait, wait wait! I have to get a mental picture of this.

OUISER. A dirty mind is a terrible thing to waste. Not that it's any of anyone's business, but no. We are friends. He would like more. I'm dealing with that. But I am old and set in my ways.

SHELBY. You are playing hard to get.

CLAIREE. At her age she should be playing "Beat the Clock." She's just like her old dog…both have trouble with their new tricks.

TRUVY. Ah! No talking trash in my shop!

OUISER. I can't help it if men find me desirable.

TRUVY. Shelby? When are you going to bring that baby of yours by?

SHELBY. Oh! I brought a picture of him. Let me show you!

TRUVY. Has he gained any weight?

SHELBY. He's about fifteen pounds now. *(Proudly showing pictures.)*

OUISER. God. He is a tiny thing.

SHELBY. He only weighed a pound and a half when he was born. But he'll catch up. Give him time.

CLAIREE. Bless his heart. Boy, those were some anxious hours, weren't they? We didn't know who to worry about the most…you or that baby.

SHELBY. I certainly wouldn't recommend having a baby three months premature.

CLAIREE. I get upset thinking about it…

SHELBY. Then let's don't. Yep. Jack Jr. is a little fighter. And he's going to wear me out. I wish I knew where he gets all that energy.

TRUVY. Don't try to do it all yourself. You get that husband of yours to help. They're supposed to be helping out this decade.

SHELBY. He helps, I guess. Mama doesn't think he does. But he does. Sometimes. When he thinks about it. Which isn't often. Most of the time he doesn't do a damn thing. And every weekend he's off hunting.

TRUVY. *(Surprised.)* Oh. But…Jackson certainly is a good provider.

SHELBY. Yes. That's true.

TRUVY. And he'll come around. And when he does, I want you to run tell me how you accomplished it. And I'll get to work on that sofa slug I'm married to. *(Truvy offers a choice of nail polish colors.)*

SHELBY. This one's pretty…

TRUVY. I thought so. Private passion is my favorite. It's luscious without being sleazy. *(Truvy remembers.)* Now, ladies? Next Saturday we have to make time adjustments. I'm going to be here all by my lonesome. Annelle is taking a well-deserved vacation.

CLAIREE. That's nice. Are you taking a trip?

ANNELLE. Yes, I am.

CLAIREE. Aren't you going to tell us where you're going?

ANNELLE. *(Directed to Ouiser.)* No.

OUISER. Please Annelle. I don't know how I'll get through the week without this information.

ANNELLE. You'll just make fun.

OUISER. Annelle. You know I love it when you go on and on about your spiritual growth. I just can't get enough.

TRUVY. She has a very nice little trip planned to Camp Crossroads in the Ozarks.

CLAIREE. I don't believe I've ever heard of a Camp Crossroads...

ANNELLE. It's in the middle of Arkansas. It's a Christian camp. There's just cabins, a chapel, a dining hall in the middle of the mountains with a lake. I will spend a week in Bible study, prayer, and meditation. You're in the middle of nature, surrounded by the beauty of the Lord.

OUISER. Are there waterbeds?

CLAIREE. Ouiser, leave her alone.

OUISER. I'm just trying to find out more about Camp Cross-eyed. I might want to go.

CLAIREE. That's a laugh. You've never done a religious thing in your life.

OUISER. That's not true. When I was in school, a bunch of my friends and I would dress up like nuns and go barhopping.

CLAIREE. Is your boyfriend going with you?

ANNELLE. No. He said he'd rather eat dirt.

OUISER. I'm going to check up on my granddaughter and make sure she's still going to the Episcopal church. This born-again process seems awfully tedious.

ANNELLE. I have to say this, Miss Ouiser. And I don't mean to hurt you. But...I worry about your faith sometimes.

OUISER. My faith is fine... (Affecting a lisp.) Ith my hair that needth the motht work.

CLAIREE. Ouiser. One of these days somebody's going to cut the feet out of your stockings.

TRUVY. Ouiser, have you no shame?

ANNELLE. Oh, that's all right, Truvy. I love Miss Ouiser. I pray for her everyday...sometimes twice. (This catches Ouiser off guard. M'Lynn enters carrying a package.)

56

M'LYNN. Morning everybody! *(Shelby's haircut hits her like a ton of bricks.)* Shelby...!

SHELBY. Mama. Please don't say anything. I like it. It'll be so much easier to deal with.

M'LYNN. Oh, honey. Bless your heart.

SHELBY. It'll dry so quick. All I have to do is run my fingers through it.

M'LYNN. The last time you had short hair was...kindergarten.

SHELBY. I know. I decided today that I'm going to get my hair all cut off every twenty-five years.

M'LYNN. I love it. I do.

SHELBY. It's not too perky, is it?

M'LYNN. It looks great. How're you doing?

SHELBY. Fine, Mama. How are you?

M'LYNN. Just fine. Here. I brought you a goodie...you can open it later. *(M'Lynn hands Shelby the package.)*

CLAIREE. M'Lynn. It must be nice having your entire family home this weekend.

M'LYNN. It's rare indeed. But it has been very nice.

TRUVY. Any special reason?

M'LYNN. Just to get together. Last week was our anniversary.

CLAIREE. Why didn't you say something to remind me? I would've baked you something. Drum loves my nut surprise cake.

M'LYNN. We've never considered it a major occasion before.

TRUVY. Which one is it?

M'LYNN. Thirtieth.

ANNELLE. Ooo! That's a big one. What is the thirtieth anniversary?

M'LYNN. How do you mean?

ANNELLE. You know...first anniversary is paper. Twentieth is china. Twenty-fifth is silver. Thirtieth must be...

M'LYNN. Valium.

TRUVY. What would Drum say if he heard you say that?

M'LYNN. Nothing. He doesn't have any idea what Valium is.

The man prides himself on never having any tension. Which is amazing considering the amount he has created over the years... Hm...listen to me. I've got to stop taking potshots at Drum all the time. He's a good man, he's crazy, but he's a good man.

OUISER. He seems to be behaving himself lately. He was most civil in the Piggly Wiggly yesterday. I was caught off guard and smiled before I could help myself.

M'LYNN. The most bizarre thing has happened. Drum and I seem to be rediscovering those things that brought us together in the first place. I don't know if we buried them or became blind to them.

SHELBY. Used to be, the thought of our parents being romantic made me and my brothers sick to our stomachs, but it's actually very sweet. It's been a lovely week.

M'LYNN. Every now and then Drum and I seem to find these moments of magic. I don't know. I don't know if I'm lucky to have what I have...or lucky to know what I have.

CLAIREE. That's too deep for me. I have to go get my tires rotated.

ANNELLE. *(She's ready to shampoo Ouiser.)* Miss Ouiser...?

TRUVY. M'Lynn. Maybe you should write a romance novel based on your recent experiences. I could help you with the dirty parts.

M'LYNN. No one would believe it. Shelby. You look a little pale.

SHELBY. *(Gently.)* I'm fine, Mama. How are you? *(Clairee takes off smock, tips Annelle, leaves money on counter.)*

CLAIREE. Well, ladies. If you're out and about this afternoon, stop by the Dixie Plaza Shopping Center. The radio station is sponsoring a summer fiesta with lots of prizes and a live band. They call themselves "Single Bullet Theory." *(Truvy is working on Shelby's nails. Truvy pushes Shelby's sleeves back to get them out of the way and sees Shelby's bruised arms...)*

TRUVY. Shelby?! What have you done to yourself?

SHELBY. Oh. It doesn't hurt.

TRUVY. What have you been doing? Have you seen this, M'Lynn?

M'LYNN. Yes, I have.

SHELBY. The doctor's just been trying to strengthen my veins. They're in terrible shape.

CLAIREE. *(Crosses to Shelby and examines her arms.)* It looks like you've been driving nails into your arms. What's going on here?

SHELBY. Shall we tell them, Mama?

M'LYNN. I guess so. No point in keeping it a secret any longer. Shelby's been driving nails into her arms.

EVERYONE. M'Lynn?!/Stop that./Be serious./What's going on?

SHELBY. It's my dialysis. *(Except for M'Lynn, the room is in shock.)*

ANNELLE & OUISER. What?

SHELBY. Dialysis. It's when…

ANNELLE. I know what it is.

TRUVY. Please tell us what's going on, honey!

SHELBY. It's not any big thing. No big thing. Don't look at me like that.

OUISER. How long have you been doing this dialysis?

SHELBY. A couple of months.

CLAIREE. Mary Lynn Eatenton! I am without words! Why haven't I been told?

SHELBY. We, uh…there was no point. Sometimes you don't want to talk about things.

M'LYNN. What would have been the point? There's nothing you could do.

ANNELLE. We could have done something.

CLAIREE. I can't believe you didn't say anything. This is selfish. This is very selfish of you.

SHELBY. Hold it. You're all talking like this is something.

TRUVY. This isn't something?

SHELBY. Having Jack Jr. put too much strain on my kidneys and now they're kaput. That's all. The doctors said this would probably happen.

TRUVY. That's all? That's all, she says…

SHELBY. I'm responding beautifully to dialysis. Do I look bad?

TRUVY. You look beautiful, but…

CLAIREE. Well? Maybe you'll let us in on what's going to happen?

OUISER. Do you do this dialysis forever?

SHELBY. I could I suppose. But that's not real convenient when you are trying to keep up with a fifteen-month-old ball of fire. So. I'll just have a kidney transplant and I'll be fine.

OUISER. Is it that easy?

SHELBY. Sure. They do them all the time in Shreveport. Three or four a week.

ANNELLE. They do. Our Sunday school class was praying for one just the other day.

OUISER. But the hard part is finding the kidney, isn't it?

CLAIREE. I saw something about it on the news. It's so dramatic. These medical teams fly all over the place taking hearts and kidneys and who knows what else. And you know the thing that impressed me the most? They carry those organs in beer coolers.

TRUVY. Stop.

CLAIREE. I would not lie in a moment as serious as this. Those doctors take out their six-packs, throw in some dry ice and a heart and get on the plane.

SHELBY. She's right.

ANNELLE. But you never know when one will pop up, do you?

SHELBY. No. I'm registered on the nationwide transplant computer.

TRUVY. How long do you have to wait?

SHELBY. There are people at dialysis that have been waiting for years.

TRUVY. That must be agony.

SHELBY. I suppose. But I'm lucky. I don't have to wait anymore. Mama's going to give me one of her kidneys. (*More shock all around.*)

EVERYONE. What?!/M'Lynn!/You're not serious!/No!/Etc.

CLAIREE. When?

SHELBY. We check in tomorrow morning.

CLAIREE. You're giving Shelby a kidney tomorrow and you haven't even mentioned it?

M'LYNN. Truvy. Please do my hair. I'm in a bit of a rush.

TRUVY. I never thought there'd ever be a time that words would fail me...but I think this is it.

OUISER. Why didn't you tell us?

M'LYNN. We just told you. We haven't known that long. We were all just tested last week. I'm the closest match.

ANNELLE. What do you mean, match?

M'LYNN. There are four categories for an organ match. I matched the best.

ANNELLE. Categories?

SHELBY. Swimsuit, evening gown, talent, and personality interview.

CLAIREE. I'm going to yank you bald-headed, smarty.

OUISER. We are very upset here.

TRUVY. I passed upset a long time ago...

SHELBY. I'm sorry. That's Tommy's joke. I think it's very funny.

TRUVY. No wonder your whole family's in town.

M'LYNN. I'm just so relieved it was me. The boys are young. I would never want them to go through it. And who would want one of Drum's mean old organs? But! The best thing about all this is that with all the tests and stuff, I have discovered I have the constitution of someone ten years younger. How about that?

OUISER. It must be so painful.

SHELBY. Not really for me. My operation's simple. Mama's is awful. They basically have to saw her in half to get the kidney. It's major, *major* surgery for her.

TRUVY. They have to saw you in half?

M'LYNN. They do it on *Circus of the Stars* all the time.

CLAIREE. This is no laughing matter!

SHELBY. Trust me, Miss Clairee. There have been more than enough tears.

M'LYNN. It'll make my waist smaller because they take out my bottom ribs to get my kidney out.

TRUVY. Cher had her ribs taken out to have a smaller waist.

CLAIREE. Please. That woman's out of her mind.

OUISER. Look. Shelby? Earlier this morning I said I'd be better off when my body wears out. I didn't mean that. You know better than to pay any attention to anything I say.

SHELBY. Miss Ouiser. Forget it.

OUISER. Well, uh…I'm a terrible person.

CLAIREE. No you're not, Ouiser. You'd give your dog a kidney if he needed one.

OUISER. Absolutely.

TRUVY. But you two seem so calm and collected…

M'LYNN. I'm happy. Look at the opportunity I have. Most mothers only get the chance to give their child life once. I get a chance to do it twice. I think it's neat. And Shelby needs her health to chase after that rambunctious kid of hers. I've got two kidneys and I only need one. I'm just glad we can get it over with before it gets too hot.

SHELBY. Ain't that the truth.

ANNELLE. I'm going to postpone my vacation a day so I can sit with your husband during the operation. I can run get Co-Colas and things.

M'LYNN. That's sweet of you…but don't change your plans.

OUISER. We'll make sure Drum has enough food.

CLAIREE. Yes. You must put your house out of your mind. We will take care of everything.

M'LYNN. I appreciate that. And I know Drum does too.

OUISER. M'Lynn. You are brave, you are brave.

ANNELLE. You know? If I didn't know better, Shelby, I wouldn't even know you'd ever been sick a day in your life.

SHELBY. That's the biggest compliment anyone has ever paid me.

OUISER. Poor Shelby…

SHELBY. *(Firmly.)* Don't say that. I have my baby. I'm very happy. If this is part of the price I have to pay, then I have to pay it. I can deal with it. *(Beat.)* Now. If I'm not mistaken, someone has a present to open.

TRUVY. *(Noticing package.)* Ooo. Is this for me?

M'LYNN. Only if you can wear a size four.

TRUVY. I can take it in.

SHELBY. *(With package.)* Mama, would you...[open it?]

M'LYNN. Sure. It's just a little something I picked up. It was on sale... truthfully. *(Shelby's nails are wet, so M'Lynn helps her open the gift.)*

SHELBY. *(Carefully holding up pink bed jacket, taking in her appearance.)* Ladies? Do I look fabulous, or what?

ANNELLE. God bless you, Shelby.

TRUVY. You're going to be the sassiest girl in that hospital.

M'LYNN. Well, what about me?

SHELBY. You ladies better come visit us!

CLAIREE. I'll be sitting right by your side when you wake up. Yours too, M'Lynn. I'll manage it somehow.

OUISER. And I'll keep Drum calm during the operation. *(She laughs.)*

SHELBY. We're in such good hands. Mama, you're going to be a while, so I'm going back to the house and spend some time with Daddy.

M'LYNN. Good. *(To the room.)* Drum's not taking this very well. He gets so emotional over the least little thing.

SHELBY. Truvy? This is probably going to gross you out, but could I have my hair? Is that too repulsive?

TRUVY. People do it all the time.

SHELBY. I had it for so long. I guess it represents an era or something. *(Shelby reaches for the long lock of hair, but her nails are still wet.)*

TRUVY. Honey...your nails...I'll put it in a box and give it to your mama.

SHELBY. I love you all! *(Shelby starts out the door. Then she comes back.)* Miss Clairee? Would you do something for me?

CLAIREE. Of course.

SHELBY. Next time you talk to Drew and Belle? I know they're upset about Marshall and all. But tell them I said that if that's the most disturbing thing that's ever happened to them...they should just get over it.

CLAIREE. I'll tell them today.

SHELBY. Truvy? Why isn't my radio playing? (*Shelby taps the radio. It plays. Shelby's fingernails are still wet. Shelby exits.*)

CURTAIN.

SCENE II

During the scene change, the song that closes Scene I fades into the following speech to denote the passage of time. It is the KPPD DJ.

DJ. (*Fading in.*) …proud of our Devils on their fourteenth straight victory and if they keep playing like this the Devils might just have another state championship to call their own. That final playoff score again…twenty-seven to six. There is no new word on the lawsuit brought by the Reverend Q.T. Bennett against the Chinquapin Parish Board of Education. The Reverend, who is pastor of the Riverview Baptist Church, has filed suit charging that the use of the devil as a mascot for our high school team encourages Satanic behavior in the youth of our community. When reached for comment about the Reverend's lawsuit, Devils head coach Waddy Thibodeaux said, and I quote, "Tell him to go to hell." (*Lights up. The radio continues to play under Truvy's phone call. It is November and is unusually cold. Clairee and Ouiser are in the chairs. Annelle is doing Ouiser's hair in silence. Annelle is visibly pregnant. Clairee is halfheartedly reading* Reader's Digest.)

TRUVY. (*On phone.*) I'm sorry honey. You know I would if I could, but I just can't today. I could squeeze you in first thing Monday. Fine. See you then, Susan. (*Truvy hangs up, then gazes out the window deep in thought. No one speaks*

DJ. My personal congratulations to Waynetta Bench of 134 Debbie Jean Drive. She is the winner of the Halloween sweepstakes sponsored in part by KPPD and Marmillion Mills. Mrs. Bench wins an all-expense-paid weekend in

for a moment. Annelle is listening to the weather report.)
ANNELLE. Thirty-nine degrees! You were right, Truvy.
TRUVY. It's too cold for this time of year, I'm gonna write a letter.
OUISER. I don't like it one bit. I turn blue when it's this cold. And blue is not in my palette.

Baton Rouge and a year's supply of plywood from Marmillion Mills…the finest plywood money can buy. If you're going out today, bundle up. We'll be doing good to get up to thirty-nine degrees. Last night was the coldest Halloween since 1948. I'm not used to this arctic weather. *(Music plays.)*

CLAIREE. Anne Boleyn had six fingers.

OUISER. Who's Anne Berlin?

CLAIREE. Anne *Boleyn*. She was one of the six wives of Henry VIII.

OUISER. I never watch public television.

CLAIREE. She had six fingers.

OUISER. What happened to the other four?

CLAIREE. She had eleven total.

OUISER. Are you trying to confuse me? What are you talking about?

CLAIREE. This article says that she had six fingers on one hand. So she had all her dresses made so the sleeves hung down to her fingertips so she wouldn't look weird.

OUISER. *Reader's Digest* is a font of useful information. *(They lapse into thoughtful silence.)*

TRUVY. *(Her scarf is tied around her neck.)* Clairee. I just love my scarf. You are so thoughtful. It really jazzes up this outfit.

CLAIREE. The only thing that separates us from the animals is our ability to accessorize.

ANNELLE. I want to spray just a little more of my French perfume. I love it so much. I love it when the smell just fills the air. *(She sprays a mist and walks through it.)*

TRUVY. Don't waste it! That stuff ain't cheap.

OUISER. Save it, honey. We're going to have to burn our clothes as it is.

TRUVY. I'm just so touched that you remembered us.

CLAIREE. I had a ball shopping. I don't care what anyone says, the French people are very friendly. And most of them had the courtesy to speak English.

TRUVY. *(Ouiser has pulled her scarf out from under her smock. It is a wild print. As Ouiser examines it:)* And I love Ouiser's, too. I may want to borrow that sometime.

OUISER. You're welcome to it.

CLAIREE. You don't like it, do you?

OUISER. It's perfect for me. A print this busy'll never show dog hair.

ANNELLE. My feet are like two blocks of ice.

OUISER. *(Sips coffee.)* This tastes like it was made in a rubber tire.

TRUVY. Annelle, remember to get that new thing for the Mr. Coffee.

ANNELLE. *(After a beat.)* Have any of you seen her this morning?

CLAIREE. I haven't. I went directly to the house when I got in. Only the boys were there.

ANNELLE. Do you think she'll come by?

OUISER. I doubt it. I'm sure her hair is the farthest thing from her mind.

TRUVY. Who knows what's on her mind. But she might need something and I just wanted to be here for her.

CLAIREE. I'm glad you decided to stay open today.

OUISER. How are the boys?

CLAIREE. As well as can be expected…

TRUVY. My husband and I are taking some barbecue over there later.

CLAIREE. I have never seen so much food.

ANNELLE. You can never have enough at times like these. My husband's back at the apartment cooking up a storm. He's convinced that his red beans and rice will make everyone feel better.

TRUVY. Maybe he's right. That's why we call it soul food. I'm gonna have to get his recipe.

ANNELLE. You'll have to ask him. Sammy runs me off whenever he starts cooking. That kitchen is so tiny he's scared he'll hit me in the stomach with a spatula.

CLAIREE. When are you moving, Annelle?

ANNELLE. Next month.

TRUVY. You had to bring it up. I can't stand it that she's moving away now that I'm about to be a semi-grandmother.

ANNELLE. It's just down the street, Truvy. A hop, skip, and a jump. That apartment is so squnched Sammy and I have to step outside to change our minds. You're toying with me, aren't you?

TRUVY. A little bit. Not a lot. Guess it's just me and the old man.

CLAIREE. Truvy. Be thankful. You'd miss him if he were gone.

TRUVY. (Chuckles.) You know? Last night, he actually got up off the couch and said, "Let's go out to eat." Well…after I came to, I asked him, "What's the matter?" I thought Deputy Dawg had been preempted. Then he said he's got a good shot at doing the electrical contracting for the new college library! I'm not supposed to tell anybody! (Everyone is excited. M'Lynn enters. No one knows what to say. M'Lynn is very together.)

M'LYNN. Hello everybody. (They all hug her.) Welcome home, Clairee. How was Paris?

CLAIREE. Perfectly beautiful. I ate too much. I brought you something pretty.

M'LYNN. You shouldn't have. (The radio is playing something inappropriate. Truvy goes to turn it off.) Don't turn off Shelby's radio. I like the noise.

CLAIREE. There's special programming today. I had Jonathan go down to the station and pull music that Shelby would have liked and they're going to play it until noon.

M'LYNN. He told me. I think you're going to be surprised at some of the stuff you hear.

CLAIREE. That's OK. It's for Shelby.

OUISER. M'Lynn. Just tell us. What can we do?

M'LYNN. Thank you. Truvy? Do you think you could work a little magic? I know I look like ten miles of dirt road.

TRUVY. Let me get my wand and my fairy dust! (*M'Lynn sits.*) How are you doing honey?

M'LYNN. I'm fine. I am a little worried about Drum. The boys got in last night. I really don't know how they're doing. Jackson is... Jackson. And he has his hands full with Jack Jr. I will admit it's hard to be somber with a baby running around.

CLAIREE. M'Lynn. I'm beside myself. Wasn't Shelby fine when I left? Can you talk about it?

M'LYNN. Oh, sure. Basically...after the transplant failed, she went back on dialysis...you knew that. She'd been doing fine the last few months. But last Monday, everything went wrong. It was like dominoes. They thought they could correct things with a little surgery. As they wheeled her down, she said, "Mama. I'm going to feel so good when this is over." They gave her the anesthetic...

ANNELLE. In a way she was right. Maybe she knew she was going to be with her king.

M'LYNN. (*A little shaken.*) Yes, Annelle. Maybe so.

ANNELLE. We should be rejoicing.

M'LYNN. You go ahead. I wish I could feel that way. I guess I'm a little selfish. I'd rather have her here.

ANNELLE. Miss M'Lynn. I don't mean to upset you by saying that. You see. When something like this happens, I pray very hard to make heads or tails of it. I think in Shelby's case, she wanted to take care of that baby, of you, of everybody she knew...and her poor body was just worn out. It wouldn't let her do everything she wanted to do. So she went on to a place where she could be a guardian angel. She will always be young. She will always be beautiful. And I personally feel much safer knowing she's up there on my side. I know some people might think that sounds real simple and stupid... and maybe I am. But that's how I get through things like this.

M'LYNN. (*Gentler.*) Thank you, Annelle. I appreciate that. And that's a very good idea. Shelby, as you know, would not want us to get all mired down and wallow in this. She would look on it as just one of life's occurrences. We should deal with it the best way we know how...and get on with it. That's what my mind says. I wish somebody would explain that to my heart.

TRUVY. Tommy said you didn't leave her side.

M'LYNN. Well. I wasn't in the mood to play bridge. *(Beat.)* No. I couldn't leave my Shelby. It's interesting. Both the boys were very difficult births. I almost died when Jonathan was born. Very difficult births. Shelby was a breeze. I could've gone home that afternoon I had her. I was thinking about that as I sat next to Shelby while she was in the coma. I would work her legs and arms to keep the circulation going. I told the ICU nurse we were doing our Jane Fonda. I stayed there. I kept on pushing…just like I always have where Shelby was concerned…hoping she'd sit up and argue with me. But finally we all realized there was no hope. At that point I panicked. I was very afraid that I would not survive the next few minutes while they turned off the machines. Drum couldn't take it. He left. Jackson couldn't take it. He left. It struck me as amusing. Men are supposed to be made of steel or something. But I could not leave. I just sat there…holding Shelby's hand while the sounds got softer and the beeps got farther apart until all was quiet. There was no noise, no tremble…just peace. I realized as a woman how lucky I was. I was there when this wonderful person drifted into my world and I was there when she drifted out. It was the most precious moment of my life thus far.

TRUVY. *(Putting the finishing flourishes on M'Lynn's hair.)* Well I don't know how your insides are doing. But your hair is holding up beautifully. All it needs is a lick and a promise. Did you have it done in Shreveport?

M'LYNN. No. I did it myself…

TRUVY. Hold it, Missy. I don't want to hear that kind of talk.

M'LYNN. Doing my own hair was so odd. I had no idea about the back…

TRUVY. You did a lovely job. I just smoothed out the rough spots. In fact. I'm going to be looking for temporary help when Annelle goes on maternity leave…interested?

M'LYNN. *(Struggling for control.)* It was just with so much going on, I didn't know if I would have time…would feel like coming here. But this morning I wanted to come here more than anything. Isn't that silly?

TRUVY. No.

M'LYNN. Last night I went into Shelby's closet for something… and guess what I found. All our Christmas presents stacked up, wrapped. With her own two hands…I'd better go.

TRUVY. *(Handing M'Lynn a mirror.)* Check the back.

M'LYNN. Perfect…as always. *(M'Lynn continues to gaze into the mirror.)* You know…Shelby…Shelby was right. It…it does kind of look like a blond football helmet. *(M'Lynn disintegrates.)*

TRUVY. Honey. Sit right back down. Do you feel alright?

M'LYNN. Yes. Yes. I feel fine. I feel great. I could jog to Texas and back, but my daughter can't. She never could. I am so mad I don't know what to do. I want to know why. I want to know why Shelby's life is over. How is that baby ever going to understand how wonderful his mother was? Will he ever understand what she went through for him? I don't understand. Lord I wish I could. It is not supposed to happen this way. I'm supposed to go first. I've always been ready to go first. I can't stand this. I just want to hit somebody until they feel as bad as I do. I…just want to hit something…and hit it hard. *(Everyone is unable to react, overcome with emotion. Eventually, Clairee has an idea. She pulls Ouiser next to M'Lynn and braces Ouiser as if Ouiser were a blocking dummy.)*

CLAIREE. Here. Hit this! Go ahead, M'Lynn. Slap her!

OUISER. *(Dumbfounded.)* Are you crazy?

CLAIREE. Hit her!

OUISER. Are you high?

TRUVY. Clairee! Have you lost your mind?

CLAIREE. We can sell T-shirts saying "I Slapped Ouiser Boudreaux!" Hit her!

OUISER. Truvy! Dial 911!

CLAIREE. Don't let her beauty stand in the way. Hit her!

ANNELLE. Miss Clairee. Enough!

M'LYNN. Hush, Clairee. *(Everyone is beginning to lighten up.)*

CLAIREE. Ouiser, this is your chance to help your fellow man. Knock her lights out, M'Lynn!

TRUVY. Clairee. You're gonna piss God off if you're not careful!

OUISER. Let go of me! *(Clairee does so.)*

CLAIREE. Well, M'Lynn. You just missed the chance of a lifetime. Most of Chinquapin Parish'd give their eyeteeth to take a whack at Ouiser.

OUISER. You are a pig from hell.

CLAIREE. OK. Alright. Hit me, then. I deserve it.

OUISER. Whatever would we do without Clairee's own special brand of humor?

TRUVY. Clairee. You are evil and you must be destroyed.

CLAIREE. Darling. Mother Nature is taking care of that faster than you could. Things were getting entirely too serious there for a moment. I'm sorry M'Lynn. We are all entitled to our sorrow.

M'LYNN. That was very funny, Clairee.

ANNELLE. I have to admit I laughed…even though that wasn't a very Christian thing to do, Miss Clairee.

CLAIREE. Annelle, honey. You're going to have to lighten up.

ANNELLE. My husband says the same thing.

CLAIREE. *(Giggles.)* I'll bet Lloyd got a kick out of that one.

OUISER. Lloyd did get a lot of enjoyment at my expense when he was alive.

CLAIREE. M'Lynn. You know how much Lloyd adored Shelby. I am sure he's up there now showing her around…fixing her speeding tickets…

M'LYNN. Shelby was always crazy about Lloyd.

CLAIREE. She worshipped the quicksand he walked on. And I'm sure when Shelby got up there, he was very happy to see a familiar face. He was a Louisiana politician. We don't know many people that went to heaven. *(Clairee turns her attention to Ouiser.)*

OUISER. Clairee.

CLAIREE. Ouiser? You know I love you more than my luggage.

OUISER. You are too twisted for color TV.

CLAIREE. Thank you.

TRUVY. Now that you two have made up, we had better let this woman go. She has to pull herself together. She cannot be a pillar of strength with eye makeup running down her neck.

ANNELLE. Go on out there, Miss M'Lynn…we'll be just fine.

M'LYNN. I shouldn't have gone on like I did. I made everybody cry. I'm sorry.

TRUVY. Don't be silly. Laughter through tears is my favorite emotion.

M'LYNN. Maybe it was about time I had an emotional outburst. Maybe I'll start having them at home more often. Drum will be so pleased. I'm so glad I came by. Shelby would've had a good time here this morning.

TRUVY. I'm sure she did.

OUISER. M'Lynn. Tell your family…especially Drum…that they've been in my prayers. *(There is a reaction from Annelle. Ouiser acknowledges.)* Yes, Annelle, I pray. There! I've said it. I hope you're satisfied.

ANNELLE. I have suspected this all along.

OUISER. But don't you go trying to get me to come out to your church to one of those tent revivals with all those Bible beaters doing God-only-knows-what. They'd probably make me eat a live chicken.

ANNELLE. *(After a calculated beat.)* Not on your first visit. *(This remark takes everyone by surprise.)*

CLAIREE. Very good, Annelle! Spoken like a true smart ass!

OUISER. M'Lynn. Owen wanted me to tell you you're in his thoughts.

M'LYNN. But I didn't think you and Owen were…

OUISER. He's coming in Monday to take me to Shelby's service. That girl will do anything to get us together.

M'LYNN. I'd better go.

TRUVY. M'Lynn. You promise you'll call if you need anything, you hear?

ANNELLE. And if her line's busy, you call me.

CLAIREE. Call me. I have call waiting. Just got it.

M'LYNN. I will.

ANNELLE. Oh! Miss M'Lynn. I don't know if this is the time or the place, but I wanted to tell you that Sammy and I decided if this is a girl, we want to name it Shelby…since she was the reason we met in the first place. If you don't mind.

M'LYNN. Mind? Shelby would love that. I'm tickled pink. (She smiles.) Pink.

CLAIREE. What'll you name it if it's a boy?

ANNELLE. Shelby, I guess.

M'LYNN. That's the way it should be. Life goes on.

TRUVY. M'Lynn. I know it hurts. But it'll get better. And if you feel like taking a whack at something…come on over and hit on me. I won't break.

M'LYNN. I may take you up on that. (To Truvy and group.) You have no idea how wonderful you are…

TRUVY. Of course we do… (As M'Lynn leaves the shop, she passes Shelby's radio that has ceased to play during the scene. M'Lynn stops, looks at it lovingly, then hauls off and gives it a mighty whack. It starts playing the theme from Hawaii 5-0 softly.* M'Lynn smiles and tells the group on her exit…)

M'LYNN. There. That's better. (Ensemble reaction. After M'Lynn's exit, Clairee takes Ouiser's hand in friendship, noticing Ouiser's need for a manicure. Annelle offers a silent prayer, which Ouiser exasperatedly acknowledges, but respectfully does not interrupt. Truvy, who has been watching M'Lynn out the window, returns to working on Clairee's hair. The action in the shop continues as the lights fade and the music swells.)

CURTAIN.

End of Play

---

* See Special Note on Songs and Recordings on copyright page.

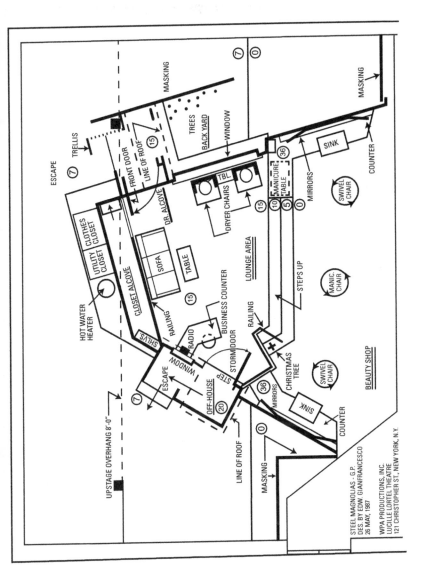

STEEL MAGNOLIAS - G.P.
DES. BY EDW. GIANFRANCESCO
26 MAY, 1987

WPA PRODUCTIONS, INC.
LUCILLE LORTEL THEATRE
121 CHRISTOPHER ST., NEW YORK, N.Y.

PROPERTY LIST

(Use this space to create props lists for your production)

SOUND EFFECTS

(Use this space to create sound effects lists for your production)

Note on Songs/Recordings, Images, or Other Production Design Elements

Be advised that Dramatists Play Service, Inc., neither holds the rights to nor grants permission to use any songs, recordings, images, or other design elements mentioned in the play. It is the responsibility of the producing theater/organization to obtain permission of the copyright owner(s) for any such use. Additional royalty fees may apply for the right to use copyrighted materials.

For any songs/recordings, images, or other design elements mentioned in the play, works in the public domain may be substituted. It is the producing theater/organization's responsibility to ensure the substituted work is indeed in the public domain. Dramatists Play Service, Inc., cannot advise as to whether or not a song/arrangement/recording, image, or other design element is in the public domain.